CONOR
MAYNARD
TAKE OFF

CONOR MAYNARD TAKE OFF

WITH JOE MOTT

'It's lonely at the top, that's why I plan to take all of you with me.'

INTRODUCTION

It's 1.30 a.m. one night in 2010 and I'm sitting in my parents' living room, hunched over my laptop, knowing that either I'm the victim of the biggest wind-up possible, or my life is about to change for ever.

My Skype account is open and I'm fidgeting nervously, hoping the person who's promised to call me isn't just a figment of my friends' imagination. Just in case it's *not* who I'm hoping for, I've made no effort with my appearance and I look a right scruff in a beaten-up old hoodie.

For what feels like the longest ten minutes of my life, I barely blink as I stare at my screen, willing it to spring into life with a call from one of my all-time idols.

Suddenly it happens. The ringing makes me jump, but the name isn't the one I was hoping for. Santos? Who the hell is Santos? I'm gutted. After all my expectations, it's just gonna be some fake thing. I answer and after a few seconds of loading, up pops a face. *His* face. This is not some random guy called Santos. It's not my mates cackling at me for being such a sucker.

Staring at me from my laptop screen, in a small living room in a house just outside Brighton, is my biggest inspiration and international superstar, Ne-Yo. The guy's won three Grammy Awards, sold millions of albums and worked with everyone from Rihanna to Beyoncé.

'Hey, man,' I say, trying to sound normal.

'Hello, sir,' he replies before getting straight to it. 'I'm a big fan,' he says. 'I've been watching your videos on YouTube – and I want to work with you.'

That was the moment that changed my life for ever.

I was seventeen and I remember it as if it was only yesterday. It was that call that put the final stamp of authority on what I had been doing. It meant I was no longer just some kid from south-east England singing cover songs and posting them on the internet, hoping I sounded all right.

Maybe, just maybe, I was actually good enough to become a recording artist.

Chapter One

ME AND MY FAMILY

I was born on 21 November 1992 and brought up in Brighton by my parents, Helen and Gary. In fact it was just outside Brighton – Hove actually, as my mum would say.

I'm the oldest of three kids. My brother Jack was born two years and two days after me and my little sister Anna is seven years younger. We're a happy family and I was always a happy little kid. From a very early age I knew I had support and love from my parents and I felt well loved.

We lived on a quiet street and everything was pretty normal really. My parents weren't well off, but we lived in a house that was just the right size for our family.

My dad's a carpenter who worked mainly in London and my mum's a civil servant at Jobcentre Plus, helping people find work. My dad would always set off for work very early in the morning and we'd go to bed soon after he got home. That meant we didn't see him as much as my mum, but he was always around when he wasn't out at work.

My mum did all the school runs and – just because she was there – she'd be the one I'd go to if I was upset or had some news to share.

Pretty much my earliest memory – I must have been about three – is of the first time I saw snow. There's a video of me playing in it and my brother Jack sitting in his baby seat squeaking, and you could see how happy we both were.

We had a tiny little concrete garden and I was kicking the snow around, ecstatic and constantly turning to my parents, saying, 'We're having fun, aren't we?' It was like I needed to confirm that we really were having a good time. I remember sticking out my tongue and trying to catch the snow on it. 'I can't catch my tongue today,' I said, because I hadn't fully mastered making sentences yet.

As little kids me and Jack were pretty close and would play together most of the time, but as we got older we started to become a bit more argumentative. I suppose that, just like all brothers, we argued and fought a lot – probably more often than we got along, to be honest! We shared a bedroom, but we'd get into little scraps mainly when we were outside in the garden or playing football, or just arguing over toys.

Even now Jack is quite argumentative, and I would say that he started most of the fights, as I'm just not a very confrontational person. But I was bigger and older, so it was always me who would finish the fights.

One day when I was six my parents sat the two of us down and said they had a surprise for us. They explained that they were having another baby. I was so excited and really happy about it. Jack was the exact opposite. 'So, I don't get a toy then?' he said, then ran off into his bedroom and cried. I'm painting Jack in a really bad light here, but he was only four, and he loved Anna as soon as she arrived.

When my mum went into hospital to give birth, we stayed with some family friends called Vicky and Paul Strong, and my mum promised to call us as soon as she'd had the baby to tell us if it was a Harry or an Anna.

I fell in love with Anna straight away when I saw her in the hospital and to this day I adore little babies. I think they are the coolest, cutest things in the world.

In the mornings when I'd wake up before school, I'd go and get my little sister out of her cot, bring her back into my room and cuddle her in my bed until my mum came in looking for her in a panic.

My parents were very close to Vicky and Paul, as they'd met when Vicky was pregnant with their daughter Ellis and my mum had just had me.

Vicky would look after me as a baby when my mum went back to work, so me and Ellis grew up together and Vicky used to always find sneaky ways to make me and my brother kiss her goodbye on the cheek when we got older!

Every Saturday without fail we saw them and we'd have Pizza Hut together and watch *Gladiators*, *You've Been Framed* and *Catchphrase*. We'd take it in turns to spend New Year at each other's houses too. Me and Ellis used to play with our tape recorder, pretending to be Brighton local radio DJs Danny and Nicky, doing all the interviews, plus I'd sing the songs. We were incredibly close and we were all like an extended family.

Then one day my mum told me that Vicky had cancer. I didn't really understand what that meant, but I just assumed she'd get better. Very sadly she didn't, and when she died I remember my stomach turned over. I fell sideways on to my mum's lap on the sofa and cried my eyes out, which to this day is the only time I've ever cried like that.

previous page
With my family

Since then we've drifted apart, because it would have been too hard for all of us to keep seeing each other with that one person so obviously missing. I drove past their house the other day and I wrestled with myself because I wanted to go in and say hello and find out what Ellis is up to. I'd love to see her again one day.

As a kid I loved New Year and my birthday, but Christmas was pretty much the best time of year for me. One Christmas my brother and me were just ridiculously excited about these Buzz Lightyear pyjamas we'd been given, pressing all the buttons all over them, even though they did nothing! We spent hours running around the room thinking we could fly.

So it wasn't like we got massive toy cars as kids: pyjamas were our best present when we were little. That was last year. Just kidding! It was ages ago.

Our Christmases were great, though, and those family traditions are still the same. While we're asleep 'Santa' puts stockings at the ends of our beds full of little presents and, though we've always tried, to this day we've never managed to catch him!

One of my best mates when I was a kid swore to God that Santa stood on his head one night – and we all believed him. So I used to leave my hand or my foot hanging out of the bed in case he nudged it, so I could get a look at him.

Anyway, we'd wake up, grab our stockings and run into our parents' room to open the little gifts inside. And every year, as we still do to this day, we'd have the same joke with our parents: 'That's it then, that's the end of Christmas. Go back to bed.'

Then we'd head downstairs to the living room and there'd be the proper presents under the tree or sometimes in our own bags. We'd see my mum's parents on Christmas Day and then my dad's on Boxing Day, which I loved too. There'd always be loads of us at the house and we'd play all kinds of games, like Uno – a card game – or a little racehorse game where you'd wind the horses up and if yours won you'd get some sort of prize.

Then we'd have a lovely Christmas dinner – and my mum's chestnut stuffing was like the one for me. I'd always look forward to that more than anything.

Unfortunately my grandparents on my mum's side have died now, so it's just us on Christmas Day, but all the routines are still exactly the same.

One of things that I really love about the success that I've had is that it's made me able to give back. People always ask me what's the most extravagant thing I've bought myself, but I actually haven't bought anything like that! I'd always much rather buy things for other people. I take far more pleasure in giving things than receiving them.

So this year I bought my brother a car for Christmas – a Mini Cooper.

I actually tricked him. I'd bought my little sister Anna a top of the range tablet to use for school and the internet and I gave Jack a much cheaper version of the same thing. He obviously had to say 'thank you', but he was clearly really disappointed. Then I gave him this little tiny box with a key in it and he looked baffled. I told him the other part of it was upstairs, but as he passed the front door to the stairs I knew he'd look out on to the driveway – and see his car!

To start with he wouldn't drive it, though, as he was too scared he was going to mess it up.

I love that I was able to do that because in the old days the best he could have hoped for from me was a jumper that my mum had bought. I'd just put my name on the Christmas card.

It was the same for my folks. I never had my own money, so my dad would get a bottle of aftershave that my mum had bought. Last Christmas I bought him one of the poshest watches out there, which was actually a bit of a problem because I'd already bought my mum a watch and then she told me my dad needed one. So they both got the same present.

I have this dream that one day I will get my dad an Aston Martin. I don't mind him knowing that now, though I'm not quite there yet. But one day…

Last Christmas I only had a week off and I hadn't seen my parents for about four months, so it was just really good to spend some time with them.

My first best friend, Niall, lived two doors down the road from us and he was a year younger than me and a year older than Jack. The three of us would play football in our back gardens, or make up little games, like pretending sticks were magic staffs and we were wizards.

There was no limit to what we'd make up for fun. One year my dad put up a zip wire in the garden that must have been about six feet long. It went from our little tree house to one corner of the garden. It was amazing and we'd do stunts on it.

And we used to swap Pokemon cards, but the truth is I never really wanted much and, since I didn't have pocket money, most of the things I'd do as a kid involved using my imagination. I'm still the same these days. I don't actually need much to be happy. If someone gave me £20 million today, I wouldn't change my lifestyle and buy a huge home for myself.

I have simple pleasures and I like simple things. As a kid my favourite meal was spaghetti hoops and mashed potato, which we used to get every Friday. And I've always loved Galaxy chocolate bars. They were used as a treat or a bribe to encourage me to do well at school, so if I'd been good and managed to win a gold star, at the end of the week I might be lucky and get a chocolate bar to say, 'Well done.'

We used to have family holidays. My mum was absolutely in love with caravan holidays, but we never went out of the UK. We'd drive down to, say, Devon and stay on a caravan site where there'd be entertainment in the evening. For our summer holiday every year we'd go to Butlins for about a week, which I loved. That was the age when a week would last for ever. My mum's got a video of me on a little Postman Pat ride singing along to his theme tune at one of the camps.

I always had an obsession with water, swimming pools and the sea. At Butlins there was a little swimming pool – this was long before I could swim – and I went steaming in and leapt into it. My dad had to jump in and rescue me. He wasn't best pleased because he was still in his trousers, with his wallet and his phone and everything in the pockets.

One time I tried to do the same thing at the beach, but because it was low tide I spent about five minutes running towards the water and actually lay down on the sand and fell asleep before I got there.

Fortunately I can control myself now. If I'm on a date with a girl and see a puddle I manage not to jump in it and start splashing about!

Chapter Two

BITTEN BY THE SHOWBIZ BUG

When I was five I started at St Mary's Catholic Primary School, which was just two minutes around the corner from my house. My birthday is in November, so I was one of the older kids in my year, which meant I had to stay there the whole day rather than go home early like the younger ones could.

Unfortunately my schooldays started off badly when, by accident, I got on the wrong side of the future head teacher, Miss Jones, in one of the first assemblies I attended. I was sitting right at the front, next to a little girl who was playing with her bead bracelet, which snapped. As all the beads bounced on the floor and rolled away, we both froze.

Then the girl pointed at one which was heading towards the teachers. For some reason I found this really funny and let out a laugh, which I managed to hide by putting my hand over my mouth and leaning forward. Of course Miss Jones clocked me and wanted to know if I was OK. 'Are you going to be sick?' she asked. I had no idea what to say and the next thing I was being taken off to see the nurse.

I ended up sitting there missing lessons and drinking a little cup of water – which was really refreshing – until break time.

At break, Miss Jones came over and asked if I was feeling better and gave me a massive hug. I thought I ought to tell her the truth, but when I said, 'I wasn't really going to be sick,' she hit the roof. She thought I'd pulled a trick to try to get out of attending assembly. From that day onwards she told me she'd keep an eye on me. I was in her bad books and she had me marked out as one of those naughty kids, which I just wasn't.

But I did get in trouble quite a lot at primary school – mainly by accident. I would just do things not realising it was going to land me in trouble. I remember once pulling a branch on a tree in the playground really hard and one of the teachers told me not to. 'Why?' I said, as a genuine question, which he mistook for me being cheeky. I had to stay behind after school and my parents were phoned about it.

My two best friends in primary school were Alex and Joey. We called ourselves 'the Gang' and we did get up to some mischief. One day Alex turned around to me and said, 'I'm not allowed to sit next to you in class any more because my mum told me not to.' The thing is, I just loved chatting and having a laugh. I wasn't exactly bad, but I did like to mess around. Joey was quite like me in that way too. I was forever being told to quieten down, but sometimes I'd get sent to the head or told to stay behind after school for doing something stupid.

Once I was put in charge of handing out all the little book bags to my classmates at the end of the day. These were stored in a tray and I was supposed to go around giving them to each of the pupils. I decided it would be a much quicker way of doing it if I just stood there and threw the bags out backwards over my shoulder for my mates to catch. Of course they just went flying everywhere and I ended up in loads of trouble.

Although my mishaps were always accidental, it was made worse because Miss Jones already thought I was a naughty kid anyway. But in general my primary-school days were pretty good and I have happy memories.

My mum had noticed that from quite an early age I loved performing, so she encouraged me in that direction a little. She told me that when I was a little boy she once took me to the doctor and while we were sitting in the waiting area I got up and stood in the middle of the room and started singing the *Barney* theme song to everyone. I just had no problem performing in front of people, whereas most kids would be shy and stick near their mums.

I was like that at primary school too. Me, Joey and Alex used to get together with a few other friends and pretend to be Blue. I was always Lee Ryan and I'd try to do all the big vocal runs and flashy scales he would sing. We'd do it in the playground for classmates. 'All Rise' was one of our best. I think I was always a little bit more into it than they were, so while I'd always want to do it, they'd sometimes be like, 'Can't we just play football instead?'

As a kid I really liked to sing. After school, me, Jack and Niall would get together in the back garden and sing the *Pokemon* theme song. We absolutely loved it and we'd take the CD player out there and put the song on repeat while we rode around on our little bikes for hours, singing the song and pretending we were actually on it. 'I wanna be the very best...' God, that's embarrassing to admit!

Aged six, while still at primary, I started going to drama school part-time. Lawrence, a kid at St Mary's, had a sister who went to a drama school in Brighton called K-BIS. My mum thought it would be a good idea to send me there because I like performing so much, so me and Lawrence started going on Saturday mornings.

I didn't really see it as school because we were so young. It was more like playtime, as a lot of the early lessons were just playing games to get us all comfortable with performing in front of a group. From the very start I just loved it. Although once again – like an idiot – I got on the wrong side of the head teacher, Marcia King, very early on.

There was a game called sleeping fishes where you had to try to catch people moving as they tried to lie still. Eventually it got down to this one girl who just would not move, so I said, 'I bet I can make her move.'

Then I walloped her right in the belly. I wasn't meaning to hurt her – I was just over excited and trying to make everyone laugh. My mum had to come down to the school and I was in real trouble, which marked me out as a bad lad with the head. I think what saved me, though, was the fact that I was actually quite good at the performance side of stuff.

But by the time I was eight I thought I'd had enough and left because I wanted my Saturdays back. I just stopped going without telling anyone. My mum wasn't too upset about it because she knew I'd have only messed around in the lessons if I wasn't interested in it, so there was no point in forcing me.

But shortly after I left, she saw an advert in the local paper saying there were open auditions for the Christmas pantomime of *Peter Pan* at the Theatre Royal in Brighton. So she and my dad suggested I go along. It was really weird because I saw some of the kids from my drama school there. One boy was just a little too tall, so they turned him away, and it made him cry.

When it was my turn they said straight away, 'No, he's too short,' but eventually they let me audition because I was literally a millimetre under the size they wanted.

The audition was to choose the Lost Boys – just little background parts really – but as this was my first audition I didn't really know what to do. We all went on the stage and had to read a bit from a script and then do a song. I think I sang part of a number from *Oliver!*

The bit that I *really* wasn't feeling was the dancing. I'd never really danced before and I thought it was for girls. Luckily I managed to wing it by doing a step ball change, which is a really simple dance move I'd learned at K-BIS.

Eventually the director started calling names from the group who were left onstage and assigning parts to everyone. When he got to my name he said I was going to play Michael. That didn't mean anything to me, as I was there to play a Lost Boy and didn't know the story of *Peter Pan*. Basically it was a much bigger part than I had auditioned for and I was ecstatic that I had got it.

When I went back to school the next day, the teacher stood me up in front of the class and told everyone I'd got the part. That felt a bit odd, but I did enjoy the feeling that other people were impressed by it too.

Michaela Strachan was the main star and we had about a month of rehearsals before it started for Christmas. It was a bit weird because there were quite a few kids from K-BIS in the show, but I had a bigger part than most of them, which felt a little awkward since I'd left the drama school.

The hardest part for me was that – what with it being Peter Pan – I had to fly, which meant having a harness strapped around my groin that lifted me completely off the ground. It was *very* uncomfortable. I got to fly, but I also had my balls crushed every night. That's helped me hit the high notes ever since!

Being backstage was one of the best bits for me, as it was basically a load of kids messing about and eating Jammie Dodgers.

One day my two best friends, Alex and Joey, came to watch the show and it turned into a nightmare. I had to walk down some steps from the stage, go in among the audience and then get back up onstage. My friends were in the higher-level seats, so I was looking up and waving at them, not watching where I was going. I fell clean off the stage in front of everyone, rolled all the way down the stairs and landed in the lap of an old woman sitting in the front row. I leapt up and carried on with the show, trying to style it out even though I'd proper stacked it.

I remember absolutely loving the feeling of being onstage from the very start. The truth is, I wasn't nervous at all. Doing *Peter Pan* made me realise that I actually loved performing, and I told my mum that I wanted to keep doing it, keep being onstage. I was pretty upset when the show finished.

We went back to K-BIS and basically begged the head teacher to take me back. She put up a fight but finally took me back, and I also signed up with the agency that was part of the school because I wanted to be put forward for auditions too.

By now I was nine, so when I went back I was in the older group and the lessons became a bit more serious, teaching us things like improvisation and stagecraft. Acting was what I really loved to do. But at this stage there was still nothing in the lessons about singing, although I sometimes used to sing in front of my classmates at St Mary's on a Friday, when the teachers would get lots of different people up in front of the class to have a laugh. I would sing Elvis's 'Blue Suede Shoes' and do my imitation of his voice for fun, which I think the teachers enjoyed more than the kids.

I kept my two school lives a little bit separate. It wasn't a secret that I went to drama school on a Saturday, but while I was at primary school I kept my two sets of friends apart. My best friend at K-BIS was a boy called Samir and if we hadn't got on so well I think we would have been enemies, as we were both pretty high up in the class. It was always one of us who would get pulled out to be used as an example and we became really good mates.

But what I was learning at drama school didn't really cross over into primary school and I think I was a different person at each of them. At St Mary's they would have had a giggle at what we did at K-BIS – having to stand up and act in front of people and stuff. Especially when I hit ten, because at that age I started to do the singing and dancing lessons too.

I only really started those because, after our drama class on a Saturday morning, I'd go home but Samir and my friends would stay on for extra lessons, and I felt like I was missing out on the fun. The only downside was that I had to wear the awful dance gear I'd always laughed at! Tight black trousers called jazz pants, ballet shoes and a tight black T-shirt.

But if I'd never bitten the bullet and put on the silly clothes, I probably wouldn't be where I am today.

Chapter Three

FIRST TASTE OF FAME
AS A SCHOOLBOY

Starting at Cardinal Newman Catholic Secondary School in Brighton was a big deal for me and a bit daunting, as there were so many new people there.

I went along with my mates Joey and Alex, but on that first day of Year Seven, when I was eleven, my form tutor made me sit next to someone completely new. I ended up next to a boy called Paul, who became one of my best friends at that school.

My mum had said that I shouldn't worry if I didn't make any friends on the first day, but by the end of the day Paul and me were getting along and he said, 'You can tell your mum she was wrong to worry!' I was really happy when he said that because it meant he considered me his friend, which I hadn't been expecting.

What I found hardest was that at primary school the Gang had been pretty much top dogs but at secondary school it was more like every man for himself at the start. No one knew anything about anyone and we were all equal again. It was a real culture shock, because even on the first day I found out about so many things that I'd never really experienced in my life before.

The older kids had to take us around and show us the ropes. They told us which banisters not to touch because people would spit on them, and where to go if we wanted to have a smoke without getting caught. Not that I was a smoker.

Later that same day I witnessed a real fight between two older girls and it was truly awful. I found it frightening and I realised that since I wasn't a hard kid I was going to have to up my cheekiness and bravado to survive.

I also met kids who would stand up to teachers, whereas at primary school there was no question of ever answering back. Paul was a bit naughtier in that way and not just with teachers. He'd stick up for me if there was any grief at all, but having a friend like him both helped me and got me into a bit more trouble as well. I started getting after-school detentions, especially for Science, a subject I hated. Paul and me would be caught chatting, telling jokes, throwing things at each other and generally being disruptive.

Discovering swear words was a big deal to me. Everyone else around me was swearing and about halfway into Year Seven I remember walking down the road and saying the F-word for the first time. It felt really weird but really exciting too and it immediately made me dread the day my brother was going to start secondary school as I didn't want him to grass me up!

As a little kid, if you swore, even your best mate would have to tell on you, to save you from yourself and being bad. But I learned in secondary that you don't snitch on people for swearing because it's not your place.

When I was in Year Eight, aged about thirteen, I got really into Parkour free running and me, Paul and another kid, Tye, would go to Hove Park School, run around on top of it and jump off things. It wasn't proper, disciplined stuff – we were just messing about – but we thought we were amazing. Like idiots, we put up a video online of us doing our little jumps and said our names on it. The school complained to the police that their roof had been damaged and the police found our video and knew it was us. We got called into the head teacher's office for a meeting with the police and were given a stern warning. I was also in serious trouble with my parents.

I made my first enemy at Cardinal Newman. Whereas before I'd always got along with everyone and we all seemed to like each other, at secondary it was a bit different. There were hundreds of kids there and there was one boy that I just didn't click with. He was the funny guy in his group of friends and I was the funny guy in my group and some of our two groups crossed over, but the two of us just didn't see eye to eye.

A boy that I knew had been chatting to this lad's girlfriend, but when the eventual confrontation took place between them, this boy told my enemy it had been *me* who'd been chatting up his missus! Then it went all around the school that this lad was going to fight me. Eventually I went up to him and asked him if he was going to try to beat me up, but he looked at me as if I was a weirdo and said no – which was good because he was massive. From then on we just stayed out of each other's way.

Year Eight was amazing because I just had no responsibility. No impressions to make, no exams to pass and nothing important to achieve.

My closest friends were my classmates Paul, Joey and a boy called Billy. We got into so much silly trouble and were always in detention after school. But we'd all be there together and it didn't stop us messing about. Eventually our head of year came into our class and told us he was going to split the four of us up because there'd been so many complaints about us from different teachers. As soon as he said it, out of nowhere this girl at the back of the room just started sticking up for us, saying, 'No, you can't move them. Please don't.' We were baffled but it worked, because the teacher said he'd give us one more chance but if there was any more messing around we'd be split up.

I asked the girl why she'd said it and she told me, 'Because this class would be *so* boring without you four in it!'

Of course the very next day Paul and Billy messed around straight away and we were all told to stay apart from then on.

I continued to make a point of keeping my drama school and my real school totally separate. No one but my few close friends at Cardinal Newman knew what I did on a Saturday because there it was all about being cool and drama school wasn't cool. Remember the jazz pants! But I loved what I was doing at K-BIS more than ever. I was still kind of top dog there, whereas at normal school there were too many people competing all the time.

I was doing a lot more singing and dancing now, but as I'd just hit puberty I was struggling a bit with the dancing. I felt really awkward about my body, and as I had no flexibility I couldn't even touch my toes.

Even though Samir and me were doing really well, the idea of telling everyone back at Newman about it was terrifying. I used to dread the thought that one day someone from my school would turn up at K-BIS and see me dancing away in tight trousers or trying to do the splits!

In singing classes we had to sing songs from the 1920s, and my mates would have taken the piss and wanted to know why I wasn't rapping Dizzee Rascal tunes or something. I still didn't really love the singing and I didn't take it seriously because I didn't think it was cool.

At thirteen I got my first proper audition and I had to go up to London on the train with a chaperone from the agency. It was for a role in a Sky show called *Dream Team*, which was all about a fictional football team.

The first day of auditions was really weird because we all looked identical. It was like a room full of clones – small, blond boys. I realised that I wouldn't be able to get by just on how I looked and that I was going to have to shine and show what talent I had.

I read some script out to them and they said they'd let me know. Off I went home to Brighton, but then I got a call on a subsequent day and had to go back up to London again. It was really exciting, but I didn't know if I had the part and this time I had to do a reading with another boy. Once again I got sent home after being told they'd let me know. Guess what? I got called back for a third time to do another reading with yet another kid.

When I'd done that, they all started talking about filming details, but they still hadn't said if I'd got the part or not.

I got back on the train to Brighton with my chaperone and when I asked her if I'd landed it, she didn't know either, but said it was looking hopeful but not to get my hopes up.

The next day at the end of school my mum picked me up and gave me a little card that said 'Congratulations' and she told me I'd got the part. The head teacher of K-BIS had rung her – the one we'd had to beg to take me back – and said, 'Are you sitting down? Conor got the job.'

For me that was really cool because it was the moment that I managed to finally get back on the good side of the teacher I'd annoyed years earlier – Marcia King, the head of K-BIS. I'd always found her very intimidating. She meant well and she had her ways of teaching but she was very strict, so I never wanted to be on the wrong side of her. Even my mum was a little scared of her!

The filming meant I got three weeks off school to shoot in London, and landing the role gave me the confidence to go into school and tell my mates all about it. It felt like justification for all the Saturdays I'd put in at drama school.

Filming was amazing. I got to meet John Barnes, but the best thing about it was that I got to talk to my mates about playing football, because a pretend football team was what the show was all about.

The thing for me growing up was that I loved playing football for fun, but I didn't follow it because my dad supported Arsenal and I supported Man United, who he hated so much that I was never allowed to watch them.

And by the time I got to secondary school I couldn't play for the school team because everyone suddenly got a lot bigger before I did. I was just too small. Plus I felt there was a pressure to behave a certain way if you played on the team – shouting at people and acting up. That's just not me.

But *Dream Team* really helped me connect with my friends over football, because it was a really cool show to be in and a lot of the kids who played for the school watched it too.

The experience also taught me that I wanted to be a screen actor, not a stage actor. I preferred the up-close, intimate feel of acting in front of a camera and I wasn't into the whole flamboyant thing you have to do for theatre.

But the best was still to come. A few weeks after filming I was called into the office to collect my pay for the job. I'd been told I was getting £500, which was more money than I could get my head around at that age. The head teacher gave me my cheque in an envelope, but when I opened it, it wasn't the amount I had been expecting. It was for £1012. It was like winning the lottery. I was rich! My mum and dad set me up a little bank account and in it went.

After that I was bitten and I knew I wanted to do it again. I even got my first taste of fame. Well, I say fame – three kids at school recognised me when the show was on telly!

With GCSEs ahead, in Years Ten and Eleven, I'd started to drift a bit from Paul, the lad I'd become friendly with when I first joined Cardinal Newman. We were placed in sets according to ability and I got put into the top sets for most of my lessons. It was always a little weird for me because as much as I enjoyed all of my stage-school stuff, the performing and acting, I was quite good at the academic work too, so I never knew which direction to really commit to.

I wasn't brilliant in Science, but I *hated* my Maths teacher. One time when I was messing around in class he said in front of everyone, 'I don't want you here, I tolerate you.' How can a teacher say that to a pupil?

But when it came to revising for the exams in all my subjects, I caned it for a couple of months to make sure I passed. I had to do it that way, because I never really did any work in class. When we were around fifteen, the others in my classes wanted to really work, but I still just wanted to mess around. That's when I met a kid called Jonas and another Alex – Alex McDonald. Alex has remained my best friend since then. Both were like me – they were clever but liked to mess around, so we kind of gravitated towards each other.

On the day of the GCSE results my mum dropped me off to pick them up and made me promise to go in and get them, then bring them straight out to her before I looked at them. So I had to ignore all my friends as I walked back out with the results in my hand, although I did have to open them before she saw them, just to check! I'd got quite a few As and A*s, so I knew she wouldn't be unhappy.

I did get a D for one subject – I can't remember which – so I called my mum from the foyer and put on a really dismal voice to say I got a D. Then I told her I got a C in something else, a B in something else and then I told her about all the As.

My mum was happy and I was allowed to go back and see my mates. We all walked out of the school and down to our favourite deli – the Good Stock Deli – to celebrate.

No matter how much I liked messing about at school, I never wanted to disappoint my mum. I still hope I never do.

Chapter Four

FINDING MY VOICE

When I was little my dad used to play Stevie Wonder and Michael Jackson songs all the time and I think that must have been the first music I ever heard. One of my favourite songs was track number eight on one of the Stevie CDs and because it had something to do with power I always called it 'Number Eight Power'! I was probably about three, but I remember that when there was a saxophone break I would scrunch my face up and pretend to be playing.

One of my aunties sometimes used to look after me when I was really young and I started saying, 'Zickon, zickon,' which meant 'Turn the music on', but she thought I was going to throw up, so she called my mum, who came rushing over to my auntie's, only to work out that I just wanted to hear some tunes. My nan, Sheila, loved Elvis Presley, so I heard a lot of his songs too.

My dad had a videotape of all of Michael Jackson's music videos, which I'd watch religiously over and over. It had all the big ones on there: 'Thriller', 'Bad', 'Billie Jean', 'The Way You Make Me Feel' and 'Black Or White'. But 'Beat It' was my favourite, because I loved that guitar riff.

At around eleven I went through a stage where I absolutely loved rock music. I was massively into bands like Good Charlotte, Green Day, the Rasmus and the Darkness. The Darkness's album *Permission To Land* was the first CD I wanted that had the 'Explicit Content' sticker on it and I had to beg my mum to buy it for me, because obviously I wasn't old enough to and it had swear words in it. I wore skater clothes, flame T-shirts, black wristbands and big, baggy jeans.

After that I got into Eminem and Dizzee Rascal, plus some Grime, so I was listening to people like Wiley – which was odd as I've since gone on to collaborate with him on 'Animal'. If someone had told me that was in my future, I'd have laughed them off the planet.

I have a very happy memory of one of my mates trying to quote a Wiley tune and getting it spectacularly wrong. I wish I'd been able to video it as he was really getting into character, strutting along and saying, 'She's stolen my Rolex.' All of us were on the floor cracking up, because it was supposed to be 'wearing my Rolex'! Now that would have been a YouTube viral!

But when music started to become an obsession for me was when I got into R&B. I properly fell in love with that genre. A lot of kids at K-BIS were always talking about Usher, Chris Brown and Ne-Yo, but I always felt a bit left out because I was into other stuff and couldn't really relate to the songs they were discussing. So I thought I should at least have a listen – which led to me buying Usher's *Confessions* and becoming almost obsessed with the album. I loved the runs and the technicality of his voice and I knew that I wanted to sing like that.

I was about fourteen then and I'd started to get into singing a bit more via K-BIS and it was something that I really enjoyed doing in my spare time. My voice had just broken and up until now I'd only really been singing show tunes and old songs at drama school, so nobody – including me – really knew how my voice sounded.

At the end of the year there was a K-BIS school show and I had a solo in it which I just couldn't sing as my voice was right in the middle of breaking. It was so embarrassing. I had to kind of speak the whole part and get through it with a red face.

But as I got more and more into R&B, I grew more confident with my voice, singing along to artists I found online, like Mario and Justin Timberlake. I would try to get that kind of sound in my voice. It was a contrast for me because my mates away from drama school weren't into that kind of thing at all. They were into harder stuff, Rap and Grime, not guys singing about girls.

But at that time I had no dreams of being a singer. For me it was still all about being an actor, as I loved that feeling of having all eyes on me that I experienced in my classes, plus I'd had that bit of success with *Dream Team*.

When I turned fifteen I had a very strange experience that sparked my journey into music. I was walking down the road with a girl called Ebony. I used to get the bus home with her after school – I kind of liked her as well, but she'd quickly put me in the friend zone – and I was singing 'Same Girl' by Usher and R Kelly. And Ebony just freaked out next to me. She was saying, 'Oh my God, you're amazing! What the hell? Did you just make that noise with your mouth?' She made me sing it again and kept telling me how good it sounded. I loved hearing it, but it was weird because I'd never had that kind of reaction from anyone about anything I'd done before.

The next day I was in school and Ebony pretty much brought all her friends over to me and got me to sing again in front of all of them. It was a bit nerve-racking being put on the spot like that, but I went for it and they all seemed to like it. The main thing they were saying was that they just hadn't expected that voice to come out of me.

previous page
With my new guitar at Christmas

For a while after that, my breaks would basically be me singing to people in the playground. To be honest, it was all girls – it would have been a bit weird if a load of teenage boys had come up to me asking me to sing for them! I can't lie: it was nice getting the female attention.

This was the first time I'd ever taken my performing into normal school, and people started to realise I could sing. It was fun, but my mates soon got sick of it and after a while it felt a bit odd that I wasn't hanging with my friends or playing football because I was singing to girls.

That's when I first thought I would start recording myself, so I could give the recordings to people and have a bit more time doing ordinary stuff with my mates. I also wanted to hear it for myself, to know what I sounded like. When you're actually singing, you're just concentrating on getting it right and you can't really tell what you sound like.

So I went home and used my webcam microphone to record some songs – the first ones were 'Something Special' by Usher and 'Miss Independent' by Ne-Yo. I would just find whatever backing tracks I could online – some were really lame – and use free recording software to patch together a song. I probably did one recording with my webcam mic, but it sounded so crap that I unplugged the SingStar microphones from my PlayStation and Sellotaped them to the end of my bedstead to make a kind of microphone. So I'd record these songs really roughly and send them to a few friends as MP3s on MSN or via email. Mainly to Ebony and a few other girls.

Then one day one of the bigger boys at Cardinal Newman called me over during break time. He looked a bit shifty as he said he knew I'd been recording songs, and I was absolutely positive he was going to start taking the piss. But he said he'd heard a few and thought I sounded really good. That gave me a real confidence boost because I was the only boy in our school doing anything like this. If I had been rubbish at it, I would have been a sitting duck, but it seemed that I was quite good, so that made it OK.

Then this girl called Katie – who was one of the hottest girls in my year – added me on MSN and said she wanted to hear some of my songs. I'd never spoken to her before – I'd just looked at her in school from a distance, like most of the other boys had! Even though she was really positive about the songs, I still didn't have the nerve to speak to her in real life, so when I'd see her in the corridor at school I'd walk the other way to avoid having to say hi. Eventually, on MSN, Katie asked, 'Are you actually going to talk to me at school tomorrow Conor?' and I knew I was going to have to get over my fear. The next day I started chatting to her and she was actually really nice and not at all intimidating, making me feel like an idiot for being nervous at first.

It's funny because basically everyone was really supportive of me in a way that you wouldn't expect kids to be. I remember watching a documentary about Britney Spears where she said that when she first started singing, kids were really horrible to her – which was completely the opposite of what I experienced.

Towards the end of Year Eleven my school life and music started to meet. It became more and more known that I could sing and I decided to get my courage together and enter the school talent show. So I went to the music room and asked the music teachers if I could audition for the show, but they didn't take me seriously at all, because I'd been known as a bit of a cheeky lad who liked to mess around – even in music lessons.

I'd missed the deadline and there were no spaces left, but they said if someone dropped out, then I might be able to do something. I was gutted, but someone did drop out, so during break I ran back and got up onstage with my backing track for 'Something Special'. The teachers were impressed enough to put me through to the show – probably because they had expected me just to get onstage and fart down the mic or something!

Friday came and most of the school turned up at break time to watch the talent show. The teachers sat on a panel like judges and it came down to me and a band to win it. But the main teacher judging was a very rock guy and he was really into the band rather than me. He gave them a straight ten out of ten and because my song wasn't rock he kind of took the mickey out of me.

'You have a really good voice, I can't knock that,' he said, 'but I could imagine you singing that song into another boy's eyes!' Then he gave me a seven and I lost the show plus got embarrassed in front of the school. Not the greatest experience for my first-ever appearance onstage as a singer.

I knew I'd done really well and pretty much everyone I spoke to about it was telling me I'd won the show and had been blatantly robbed.

Fortunately things got a lot better at the very end of Year Eleven, when there was a big end-of-year performance where people could do whatever they wanted. They also gave out funny awards and trophies and, funnily enough, I got the awards for both Most Likely To Be A Singer and Most Likely To Be An Actor.

I was due to sing a really unknown Ne-Yo song called 'Empty Frames' with a girl who was in the year below me, but the night before the show she texted me to say that she'd changed her mind and didn't want to perform any more. Which left me in a right state at such short notice!

But it actually all worked out well for me because I chose to sing 'Chasing Cars' by Snow Patrol on my own. As I performed it everyone in the school was singing along. By the end of the song the entire stage was covered with our whole year singing it.

After that song a girl I knew came over to me and said that lots of the other girls in the school were talking about how hot I was now. That was a big bonus for me, as teenage boys spend pretty much all their waking moments thinking about girls. Maybe this music thing might be for me after all!

Chapter Five

ONE MILLION VIEWS

After my stunning loss at the school talent show and my redemption on the last day of Year Eleven, I got quite a lot more people asking me to send them MP3s of me singing and I decided to find a better way of sharing my music. I wanted to get it out there to a wider audience. People at school liked it, my mates liked it, but I still didn't really know if I wanted to make music the main focus of my life.

My parents were always a bit wary when I said I was getting into singing, because I never let them hear it and they didn't want me to embarrass myself.

We'd watch *The X Factor* and see these delusional people who thought they were something special just because they'd sung to their mum and dad and been told they were amazing. They'd sound like a cat being strangled, yet genuinely believed they deserved to have a massive career in the music business.

I decided Facebook would be a good place to start opening up my singing to a few more people. It was still only going to be my friends, but it meant any of them would be able to listen and comment.

I wanted the sound quality to be a bit better too and my home-made SingStar mic was almost broken, so I did loads of research on the internet and found the mic that I wanted and some really cheap recording software that altogether cost about £300. I asked my mum if I could have it all for an early birthday present and after some persuading she said yes.

The day I bought my mic and first plugged it in I thought I had got a broken one because I could not work out how to get the sound to come out of both sides of my headphones. But after some fiddling about I worked it out and was soon getting recordings that I felt confident enough to post up direct as Facebook videos on my wall. The video would just consist of the title of the song and my audio track underneath it. Obviously on Facebook there was no way of knowing how many views I was getting, but I'd get a few 'likes' and a few encouraging comments from friends, plus sometimes one from a person I didn't even know but who was a friend of a friend.

While I'd been doing my research for microphones on YouTube, I'd found a handful of people who were recording cover songs and posting them up. It was nothing like today, when everyone is posting up songs. So I thought it would be a good idea for me to join in and post my own contributions too. It would be a really good way of finding out if I was any good or not. I could get a view count, it would be open to people all around the world potentially and it wouldn't just be my friends telling me what they thought.

Now here's something that not many people know – I'd already had a YouTube channel for quite a long time when I started posting cover songs on it. I started it at about thirteen, to upload dumb videos I'd record with Niall, Paul and Alex. My YouTube channel has one of the most embarrassing names for a channel ever – skillzaishereboooya. I have no idea why I chose that name apart from the fact I probably just thought it was cool. I mean, my first email address was conor-cool-dude@hotmail.com – which should give you some idea of where my head was.

So I've warned my little sister Anna to choose an email address she can actually keep, because if you come up with a silly one, you are going to have to change it one day and it's the most annoying thing ever.

Anyway, the very first video I ever posted on YouTube was called 'Cheesy Runner' and I was the cameraman – I wasn't even in it. It followed Niall around the back garden running in slow motion and was the forerunner to such classics as 'Bad Golfer', which showed people how to play golf badly and got an amazing forty views!

The very first song I ever put up on YouTube was 'Breathe' by Lee Carr, who wasn't a massively well-known artist, but I'd found him and his song online. Someone had done an instrumental of the track, which was an absolute blessing as I really didn't think I would be able to find it. For the video, I put the song up with just a picture of me singing into the mic. Nothing really happened. I got a couple of hundred views and a comment every now and then, but they were comments from people I didn't know and that was cool because they did seem to be liking it.

That was the start of my new hobby. Recording covers kind of overtook my life at this point. I'd done my GCSEs and was now in the sixth form studying Geography, Media Studies, Music Technology and IT, but I would just finish my lessons, rush home and start recording, or checking out new songs to cover on the internet.

I had no big plan to get millions of views, or become famous, and in fact I didn't even know that was something that you could do. I just wanted people to hear my music and comment on it. I'd get really excited when I had a comment and I actually got brave enough to show my mum my covers.

That basically became my life and I spent the next few months recording covers and posting them up, still only getting a few hundred views and a few comments, but loving the whole experience.

It occurred to me that I should start maybe trying to collaborate with other people, or get a girl involved. So I went a bit different and did a cover of a song by Mario called 'Crying Out For Me' with a girl from Brighton I knew called Beckie Eaves. After I uploaded it I started to get noticed around Brighton. It seemed like a lot of people in the town had heard it and we got about 10,000 views, which was an absolutely huge amount as far as we were concerned.

Soon after I'd posted it up, I was sitting in Subway and this girl who was in there that I didn't know was giggling and then started playing the song on her phone. That was the first time I'd ever been recognised in this way, and it was when people around the area started to know me as that kid who did covers.

It was around that time that I put my first original song up on YouTube. I'd written a few before but my dad had always warned me not to put them up because he actually thought someone might want to steal them! It was called 'I Love You' and I wrote it for a girl I was seeing at the time. We'd fallen out and I felt bad about it, so I wanted to try to make up for it. The song was only really short, like about a minute and a half long, but she really liked it, so I decided to make it public.

Unexpectedly some rapper from America heard it – a kid called Bun2Tha B – and got in touch via YouTube to say he wanted to throw a verse on it. I was totally up for it and this was the first time I'd done any kind of collaboration with someone from overseas, but we still only got a few hundred views when the new version went up.

I carried on doing my little covers and collaborations and then I got a message from another American rapper. This one was called Anth and he lived in Virginia. He said he wanted to get on a song with me. What caught my attention was that he mentioned that my recording and production sounded really good.

So I checked out his channel with my brother Jack and we were both blown away. We thought Anth was amazing. He was doing proper little videos of his own stuff and Jack was like, 'You *have* to do a song with this guy.'

It's really funny, though, because I still say to this day that if I'd done the song with Anth that I originally wanted to do, I wouldn't be where I am now. We were going to do some random song from a Chris Brown mixtape that no one has ever heard of called 'Pretty Girls'. So there I was trying to record it, but it was a bit high and I was struggling.

While I was working on that song, Usher brought out 'OMG' and everyone at college was hounding me to record it. So I got sidetracked from 'Pretty Girls' and recorded all of my parts

– which were Usher's parts – but then there was the will.i.am section. I didn't know any other male singers, so I wasn't really sure what to do.

Then the penny dropped. Get Anth to record a verse on that bit. He was keen and loved the idea, so he sent me his verse, I dropped it on the track with my vocals and uploaded it on to my channel as usual with a photo of me and the track title with his name next to it.

A few weeks later Anth got in touch again and said he really wanted us to make a video for it to re-upload. Just the two of us standing there lip-synching our parts into the microphone and looking into the camera. I borrowed my mum's digital camera and since we didn't have a tripod I had to use a stack of books to get it up to the right height.

I sent Anth the video I'd made and he chopped that together with his video and we put my track underneath it, which he then posted up on his own channel. I thought it looked really cool and I was happy with it, but thought no more about it for a while.

A few weeks later I looked up the video and my jaw hit the floor. I couldn't believe it because it said 100,000 views. I refreshed the page a few times because I was sure there was a mistake or I was on the wrong page, but it was real! There were loads of 'likes' and comments as well, all really positive.

After that, Anth and I swapped a lot more emails and Facebook messages and started to get a lot closer. And I began getting a few adds on Facebook from people I didn't know from Germany, Australia and all around the world.

Anth and me talked about potentially doing another collaboration to see if that video's success had just been a one-off and then he got a message from a girl called Maribelle Anes saying she wanted to collab with us. She was in Australia and she had about 25,000 YouTube subscribers, so as far as we were concerned she was a *big* deal on there. That's a lot of fans. She was YouTube famous.

Now there was a website I'd found which I used to check up on all the time called RnBUncovered.com and it showed all the new big songs that were coming out or just about to be released. One of those songs was 'Beautiful Monster' by Ne-Yo. It was going to be the first single off his new album and I listened to it and thought it was amazing.

Unbelievably someone had done an instrumental of it already, so me and Anth recorded our parts and both felt that this could be the right song for Maribelle to jump on with us too.

She loved the track and recorded her bits of video and vocals, which she sent to me and Anth. Annoyingly she'd recorded the wrong bit of the song, so I had to find a way to make it fit over a different part of the track, but we made it work.

We uploaded it to Anth's channel, because he had a lot more followers than me.

Magic happened. It was as if we'd just timed it right and all the stars had aligned or something! That was the first video I'd ever done to hit one million views. And it only took a couple of weeks to do it.

This time Anth and I had been watching in constantly, wondering how far these insane views would go and seeing the count getting closer and closer to a million. When we hit it we were so happy because it meant we weren't just a fluke the first time around.

That's when my Facebook started going completely mad and I was getting over fifty friend requests a day from people I didn't know, and constant comments on my wall. The only gutting thing for me was that because we'd put the video on Anth's channel, I wasn't getting all those views and YouTube comments. But it was obviously me in the video and no one could take that away from me.

All this singing and uploading covers had a real effect on my life at college and I was known as a singer. I was also friends with most of the good-looking girls there and had a lot of people wanting to hang out with me. Life was good and I was starting to think that singing was something I might be able to have a real go at.

But there was also a darker side as I started to see who my real friends were and who the people were that were making jealous comments. People from my school would start answering my fans on my Facebook wall in a way that I didn't like, but if I'd said anything to them at school they'd have thought I was being cocky.

Some of the kids in my lessons would pretend to be mad, screaming fans when I'd walk in, just to take the piss out of me, which was annoying. I heard about one kid telling everyone that the only reason my songs sounded good was because I auto-tuned everything and that I couldn't really sing. I know that I didn't change at all or become arrogant and I'm just not the kind of person to act big-headed. I kept my head down and ignored people who were like that.

I didn't even give my videos a big push or anything. I would post them up and tell people once they were out there. I hate people that spam everyone with stuff like that.

If it's good, it will get the views.

Anth and I carried on doing covers and we did this thing where if we pulled anyone else in on a track with us, we'd make them the centre of it to kind of showcase them. We thought it was a nice gesture. We were trying to get a new cover out every two weeks and we were consecutively hitting big views of up to a million.

I just felt like I'd got lucky and that was it, but it didn't mean anything huge to me. I thought, it's just YouTube. I still didn't make the connection in my head that this could actually lead to and create a real career in music.

I also didn't know that a catastrophe was just around the corner.

Chapter Six

YOUTUBE BLOWS UP

A little while after we'd started getting those big views on YouTube, I got a Skype call from Anth and he was almost in tears. We talked all the time about what cover to do next and how we could switch it up to keep people interested, but this was the most emotional I had ever seen him.

He told me that his channel, Anth703 – where we had been posting all our videos – had been hacked and he no longer had access to it. We were devastated and tried desperately to get the channel back, as we felt like the bottom had dropped out of our world. We emailed YouTube but got no response and we were pulling our hair out. The password had been changed, so Anth couldn't access any messages that people would send him on his channel, plus all the comments had been disabled. Even worse, it meant we couldn't upload any new videos to it.

Soon our greatest fear was realised. Whoever had hacked our channel posted loads of foreign adverts all over our videos, which meant there was potential that they would get taken down by YouTube or that the channel would be banned.

Then the worst thing happened. 'Beautiful Monster' got deleted. Our biggest success, the one that had first taken us to a million views and far beyond, was no longer in existence – just wiped away. That was the video that had really got us noticed and even led to the pair of us doing a Skype interview with a tiny radio station somewhere in the north of England.

So, after lots of soul-searching and pondering, we decided we'd just have to bite the bullet and start a new channel. We'd built up about 20,000 subscribers on Anth's channel, so when we opened up the new one we hit Facebook to tell everyone we'd started up and to come and subscribe to us again. From those 20,000 subscribers, about 300 moved over and we were convinced our moment of glory was over. How could we possibly do it again? There was no way we thought we could build up that level of awareness from scratch.

We called the new channel AnthMelo – Anth's full name – because we had it in our heads that posting on his channel was our lucky charm, so we didn't want to mess with that.

But there was a silver lining. I'd found out through that website I mentioned that Rihanna was about to release 'Only Girl (In The World)', so we got our heads down and recorded a cover of it. We did the video the same way, with me wearing a red checked shirt and Anth wearing a blue one, because we thought it would look cool.

It was posted on Anth's new channel – and it turned out we didn't need to worry about people finding us. In no time at all we got almost ten million views, which was ridiculous. It just went crazy, hitting a million in something like a week and carrying on rocketing up with viewing figures and 'likes'. People would be searching for the original song, find our version, 'like' it and then share it, making the video a viral success.

I think that's when we finally started to fully believe that what we were doing was good. The 'like' bar was massive and there was only a tiny little 'dislike' bar, so it wasn't as if people were watching it and sharing it because they thought it was so bad that it was good.

It was funny because all the comments were saying they were amazed at how many views we had got with the first video we had ever uploaded, not knowing that of course this was just our new channel!

It also gave me the confidence to start doing covers on my own and posting them to my own channel, which soon started getting good views as well. I did Mario's 'Lay In My Bed' and a piano version of 'Use Somebody' by Kings of Leon. But to this day my biggest cover was Chris Brown's 'Next To You', which I did with Ebony Day (no, not the same Ebony I went to school with!) and is now on over eleven million views. Ebony's just won the MTV's Brand New For 2013 in fact, the same thing I won in 2012. It's a small world!

I think when you start getting that many views it's inevitable that you're going to get attention from the music industry. But at the time I didn't know that. I've since found out that quite a lot of different people from labels, plus producers, had seen my videos. I started getting messages from people claiming to be managers or promoters or whatever and I tended to ignore them, not out of rudeness, but mainly just because I had no idea who these people were or what they did.

But then I began receiving quite a lot of messages from a guy in Los Angeles who seemed really keen and the fact that he was in LA definitely caught my attention. I won't mention his name because things didn't work out, but he said he worked with one of the guys from a group called Bone-Thugs-N-Harmony and wanted to do something together. He wanted to fly me out to LA and get me to meet loads of people – and then he sent me a management contract, which seemed a bit weird.

Me and my mum sat in my bedroom looking at it and scratching our heads, not really sure what we were supposed to do with it. A civil servant and a seventeen-year-old schoolboy hadn't exactly had a lot of training when it came to legal documents from bigshot music industry people in America!

By coincidence, my dad was doing a job for a lawyer in London at the time and he asked him for a little advice on what we should do. The lawyer passed on a number for a music lawyer called Chloe Wright, so my mum called up, feeling a bit awkward, and explained that I had a channel on YouTube and had a management contract to sign that we didn't understand. Chloe searched me on YouTube and got back to my mum pretty quickly to tell us not to sign the contract as she thought I could get a lot better if I played it right.

But before I'd really had a chance to process what Chloe meant, everything became a lot more complicated. I got a message from someone claiming to represent Ne-Yo, saying the man himself was a big fan.

In just a few months I'd gone from hoping more than a few hundred people would watch me singing a song into a camera in my bedroom, to being pursued by at least one and possibly two serious people. I say at least one because, if I'm totally honest, I didn't really believe that Ne-Yo had heard of me. I really thought it was just a wind-up or a straight lie.

This couldn't be for real – could it?

Chapter Seven

HELLO NE YO,
HELLO RECORD DEAL

Chloe thought I had a really good chance of being signed by a major record label and asked my mum if she could put out a couple of feelers to some of her contacts.

At this point I was still seventeen and had started my second year in college, but I was already starting to think that it might make sense for me to leave college if I was going to pursue music properly now.

I spoke to Ne-Yo's management a few more times as well and even had a phone call with someone, but they were a little flaky. They'd say loads of positive stuff to me, but then I wouldn't hear from them for three weeks.

In the meantime Chloe had been getting some good feedback, so I went up to London on the train to meet her for the first time. Then she could explain what her plan was and talk me through the responses she'd been getting from the various labels and managers she'd been contacting.

Of course – sod's law – it was while I was in London with Chloe that I got a text asking me if I was available to go on Skype to chat with Ne-Yo. *Right now!* I couldn't believe it. After the conversations I'd been having with these guys in America, not really believing Ne-Yo was involved, I was now going to miss my opportunity to speak to him. I explained I was away from home and they said Ne-Yo was going out now, but might be available to talk later on.

That evening I texted back to say I was ready to Skype if he was, and they said he might be around later. Eventually my folks went to bed and it was just me left, sitting downstairs with my fingers crossed, but at the same time thinking this was some sort of big hoax.

Kids from Hove don't get calls from international superstars because they've uploaded on to the internet some songs they've sung in the bedroom.

But Ne-Yo did call – and it was one of the most surreal experiences of my life. You have to remember this is one of my biggest musical influences, a true icon to me, beamed into my living room via Skype. I'd pre-ordered his *Year of the Gentleman* album before it came out and woke up early so I could download it from iTunes to listen to it before I went in to college. That album is one of my favourites to this day.

So when his face popped up, I just had to do everything I could to keep my cool. I remember thinking to myself, whatever you do, just don't look weird, just be normal. For me, very often when I meet my own fans they tend to scream in my face and get really excited – I'm pretty sure if I had done that, Ne-Yo would have just hung up. He told me he loved my voice and really liked my tone and actually said the words 'I'm a big fan.'

Now his people had been really complimentary about the cover of 'Beautiful Monster', which was me, Anth and Maribelle, so I assumed he was interested in us as a group. Which meant I was a little surprised when he told me over Skype that he wanted to sign me to his label as a solo artist.

I couldn't tell you how long that conversation went on – probably only about ten minutes – but it was the best ten minutes of my life. At one stage I actually sneakily used my phone to take a photo of his face on the screen just to prove to my mates – and probably myself – that he really had called.

The chat finished with me basically saying I'd *love* to be involved with him and Ne-Yo saying that I would hear from him very soon.

I was absolutely buzzing, but it was about 1.30 a.m. so I couldn't wake my mum up or tell anybody. I just had to go to bed. It was awful! I didn't sleep at all. That was the first time I'd spoken to anyone who was a serious part of the music industry and a genuinely big player.

The next morning I told my mum all about it. She congratulated me – then told me to eat my breakfast and go to college. What else was there for me to do, I suppose? When I got to Cardinal Newman, I told one person and within the hour the whole place knew – even other colleges knew and people were texting saying it was all lies. I tried to show people the picture, but it was a rubbish shot and it didn't even look like him, so hardly anyone believed me.

Of course it was great news for my lawyer Chloe, and when my mum told her, she explained that this would really help get other people in the industry to take an interest in me. When Chloe started mentioning to people that Ne-Yo wanted to sign me, my life got quite hectic and I ended up missing quite a lot of college as I was going up to London every day for meetings with different people.

I met a lot of record labels and got on with a couple of them, but Parlophone totally stood out to me as soon as we all met up. I was with Chloe when we met Miles Leonard, the president of the label, and Elias Christidis, the guy who became my A&R, and there was a rapport between us. We looked at some of my YouTube videos and they were really cool. They told me they believed in me but they weren't too over the top at our first meeting. They were positive without blowing smoke up my arse.

A lot of the other labels I had met spoke to me more about the business than the actual music, talking about 'building my platform' and asking, 'Where do you see your music fitting in the market?' I just wanted to make music.

I had felt a bit worried about having to go in and sing in front of the Parlophone guys in just an office, but of course with my videos on YouTube they had already seen and heard what I was like, so I managed to avoid that awkward situation.

A few days later I went back for a second meeting with them and I'd dressed myself up in mustard-coloured chinos and a shirt to try to look smart. I'd also bought myself a hot chocolate on the way in, so when I was chatting away excitedly to them and waving my hands about, I managed to spill it all down the front of my trousers without realising. I felt a right idiot in the toilet trying to clean it off and then coming back out with a big wet patch on the front of them.

I was convinced I had blown it by being utterly uncool and so I wasn't feeling brilliant when Chloe and I left the building to head back for the train to Brighton.

But while were in the cab Chloe got a text from Miles saying, 'We love him, we're going to put in an offer to sign him to Parlophone.' That was very exciting for me but it was also a bit of a worry because in the back of my mind I still had Ne-Yo and his offer to sign me, even though he'd still not actually given me a real, physical offer to sign with him at Compound Entertainment.

Chloe really did a great job and stressed that it was important for me to choose who I wanted to manage me before I signed a deal with anyone.

I'd been having meetings with lots of people who wanted to steer my career for me, but it was only when I met Sarah Stennett and Aaron Hercules that something clicked.

Aaron was – and still is – pretty much the coolest guy I've ever met and he really shared the same ideas as me about where I wanted to go with my music. We also have very similar musical tastes.

I met Sarah for the first time in the living room of her house and we talked about her kids which showed me that she was used to being around young people and knew how our minds worked. She told me some stories relating to the artists that Turn First work with and the reality of the music business.

One of Sarah's stories (which was confidential and told to me under pain of death!) really hit me hard, showing me just how well she looked after her young artists and how willing she was to fight for them.

I signed up with Sarah and Aaron pretty much straight after that and then we had to work out how we were going to handle the decision of picking between Ne-Yo and Parlophone to sign with.

Of course the day that Parlophone's actual offer came in was also the day that Ne-Yo's people got in touch with an offer too. My phone rang and it was an American number I didn't recognise. It was Ne-Yo's manager, Tishawn, with the news that Ne-Yo was in London – and wanted to meet me today!

It was a tricky one because I'd just had this great offer in from Parlophone, but how could I turn down the opportunity to meet up with Ne-Yo?

I headed over to the Mayfair Hotel and phoned the number they'd given me when I got to the lobby and was waiting for Chloe to turn up for the meeting.

This really gruff American voice answered the phone and said, 'Conor? Whut chu wearin'?'

I was like, 'What?' Why did Ne-Yo's assistant want to know what I was wearing? What was about to happen to me?! But he only wanted to know so he could find me in the busy lobby to bring me upstairs.

Chloe hadn't turned up yet, but I didn't want to look uncool telling Ne-Yo he'd have to wait for me, so we took the lift up without her.

Now I hadn't really had any experience of posh hotels, and I'd never met a superstar, so I didn't fully grasp the concept of how they roll when they are away from home.

I thought we would get out of the lift, walk along a few corridors and then knock on the door to the room Ne-Yo was staying in. But he was in the penthouse suite, so the lift actually opened right into his apartment and he was standing about six feet away from the lift doors talking to some other people.

I went and sat down on my own on the couch and when Chloe arrived, Ne-Yo came over and we started chatting – which felt like some sort of crazy dream. I'd never met a celebrity before and now here I was having a conversation with one of the biggest stars on the planet, who was also one of my idols. I'll admit that I was a bit starstruck.

I felt completely out of place – some kid from Brighton sitting in a massive hotel room with Ne-Yo and all of his American crew. But they were really cool to me and made me feel at ease. It was a really chilled conversation, just talking about music and funny videos on YouTube and there was no real business talk at all.

When the chat came to an end, Chloe and I left and she said she thought it had gone really well, but I was still in a bit of a daze.

Just like with the Parlophone call, as soon as I was in the taxi I got a call but this time it was from Tishawn, saying, 'Yo, man, what was it like meeting Ne-Yo? You ready to be a superstar?'

He told me Ne-Yo wanted to meet me again the next morning and that I needed to be in London by 10 a.m. to sit down with him.

I went back in the morning, this time with my manager Aaron, and we had a very different meeting. There was a big guy with a film camera standing outside the lift and filming me from the second I got out. Ne-Yo sat me down and was much more businesslike. He explained that he was really interested in me and would like to sign me, but that he didn't like to sign anyone without getting an idea of how they could sing live. So would I mind singing in front of him, his crew and the camera right now?

Fear struck me straight away. I'd been travelling up to London for two hours and I hadn't been expecting to have to sing anything. On the journey I'd been listening to Bruno Mars, so I just stood up and winged it by singing the chorus of 'Nothing On You'.

I looked over at Ne-Yo and he had this little smile on his face as he turned to Aaron and said, 'Yeah, I wanna sign your boy.'

Two offers in two days! This was a bit of a beautiful problem to have, because I had a great offer from a label I really had a connection with, but then I had Ne-Yo – one of my idols and a big name – also saying he wanted to give me a record deal.

Chloe, Aaron and I sat in a café across the road weighing things up and decided we'd wait until Ne-Yo's actual offer came through, so we could make a decision based on all the facts.

When it came a few days later, it didn't make matters much easier. Both offers were so appealing but I could only choose one. In the end it came down mainly to location. I was only seventeen and if I'd signed with Ne-Yo I'd have had to move away from my family and live in America.

It was really hard telling Ne-Yo 'no thanks' and I was terrified that I would upset him and never get the opportunity to work with him. I got an email back saying they completely understood my decision and wishing me all the success in the world, with the assurance that Ne-Yo would love to work with me on my music.

When I went in to sign with Parlophone at their office within EMI, it was great but a little odd because at seventeen I was just a few months off being able to sign an adult contract, so I had to get my dad to sign one with me to run just a month, before I could re-sign on my own.

I had a big meal with my label and my management and met everyone who I was going to be working with and I was given a bottle of Bollinger champagne.

That was in October 2010, just a month before my eighteenth birthday. It was the tenth month of 2010 and ten has always been my lucky number.

I think it's fair to say 2010 was a *big* year for me.

Oh, and I passed my driving test as well.

Chapter Eight

SEARCHING FOR A SOUND

I left the sixth form at Cardinal Newman shortly before I signed my record deal – at the start of my second year, just after my AS levels. It was a bit of a risk but I sat down with my head of year and talked through what was happening with the attention I was getting from record labels.

I was missing a lot of college by going back and forth to London and I really didn't want to get kicked out because I wanted the opportunity to go back to my studies if it didn't work out for me with music. Luckily my teacher was onside and recognised what an amazing opportunity this was for me, telling me to go for it as they would always welcome me back if things went wrong for me. The funny thing is, I remember people I knew at college thought I was mad.

I went into my last ever lesson there and when I told people why I was leaving, they gave me funny looks. They were like, 'Don't really get that, but OK.'

Since then I've spoken to people and they've explained that everyone basically thought I was being an idiot, throwing away an education and a good life to chase an impossible dream of being a singer. They saw me as a kid from Brighton, so therefore I had no right to expect to achieve anything in the music industry. It was as if I was jumping into some fantasy land. Just Conor who sings a few songs but isn't going to be some famous star or anything. Get a grip!

I kind of know where they were coming from if I look back at it, as it was such an important moment of my educational life. How I did at A levels would have defined my future and maybe allowed me to go to university – which was something I really wanted to do.

So while everyone else was talking about sending off their applications to uni, I was saying, 'Yeah, I'm gonna go and sing.' That's one thing I do feel sad about – I know I really missed out on the uni lifestyle. I would have probably studied Geography or Archaeology if I'd gone, but not music. I liked the idea of becoming a professor!

I started recording my first album – eventually called *Contrast* – in January 2011, several months after I had signed my deal. I had done a few sessions before Christmas, hopping on a train to London, just to get an idea of being in the studio, but it was nothing like the whirlwind of work I had been expecting.

I asked my A&R man, Elias, if it was always going to be as slow as this and he said, 'Just wait until January, mate, you will be in sessions every day of the week!'

And he was right. In the new year I'd get on a train on Monday morning with my little suitcase and walk into my first session looking like I was going on holiday. I had a few pairs of pants in there and some socks and that was about it. I'd spend all week in London, staying in the K West Hotel every night, and then go back to Brighton on Friday.

That was a pretty lonely period as I had no friends in London at that time. It was horrible. I'd sit in my room at night all on my own, I'd have breakfast alone in the morning downstairs and I'd spend my evenings watching the TV alone. I'd be really happy when the hotel added a new film to their channels because I had already watched every single film they had!

This was the first time I realised how much the life I had chosen could affect my friendships. Days of the week mean nothing in the music industry. You could have Wednesday off and be working on Saturday and Sunday, which meant that when I went home and my mates wanted to go out on Friday night, I couldn't because I had to work the next day. That downsized the number of people I spoke to, because I suppose I had less to offer as a friend. I was nearly always away from home and even when I was home, often I wasn't able to hang out.

And I found it really difficult to get people to understand why it was taking so long. People thought I had failed in my aims, because I'd gone off to sign a record deal six months ago and they still hadn't heard any of my songs on the radio. Some people were calling me a flop.

Even my mum and dad couldn't get their head around the process. My mum would be like, 'But we love that demo song you played us. Why can't they just put that on the radio?' It was so hard trying to explain to them that this just isn't how it works.

No one understood and it made me too start to doubt it was ever going to happen. All I could cling on to was the thought that there was no one in the UK that was like me as a singer. Who would I be up against? The only guy even close was Olly Murs, but he was so different to me with his voice and his vibe.

I hadn't written any songs that I liked, but I just remember believing that when I eventually released something, people would like it. Plus I still had a loyal set of fans – probably about 50,000 people on Twitter – who kept me believing it would work. I used to tweet to them when I was on the train about fun stuff on the way to and from London, trying to keep them entertained and involved and let them know that I was working. With all my time spent in the studio, I recorded hardly any covers and it was important to keep them in the loop as they'd supported me from the start.

I remember praying that my label would suddenly say they loved all the songs I'd been working on and that the album was ready so we could start releasing songs and I could go home! But I knew that wasn't going to happen as I wasn't feeling any of my early tracks and neither were they.

For me, those first months of recording were weird, because I'd always been a bedroom-recording guy. The worst bit for me was having to sing in front of random people I didn't know – producers and writers at the studio. I'd go into the vocal booth and just belt out a song, worrying about them thinking I was rubbish. Or I worried that I might write a lyric and they'd all laugh at my ideas.

In my bedroom I'd done my covers, but if I messed up there was no one to see and I could just start again. This felt different and a bit intimidating. It actually made me a worse singer because I had my way of singing and I'd hold back in the booth to make sure I didn't hit any bum notes. I remember sitting there and saying to people, 'Oh no, I don't sing that note and I don't do that kind of run!' I actually started wondering if they'd let me record in my bedroom and send them my vocals. I was so used to singing my own way that I was scared of doing anything outside of my comfort zone, and I'd just been thrust into writing and recording original material for the first time ever.

But gradually, as the sessions went on, my confidence built up and I did eventually relax. I began to get friendly with some of the writers I was working with too, which made things much easier. One of the first was Paul Lewis, who was really cool, and I'd have him in a lot of writing sessions with me. The Invisible Men were always my go-to guys as well. They really were my rock.

Even so, of all the things I wrote and recorded in the first six months of my life as a signed artist, not one was ever used. It was hard finding the right sound for me, as right from my early YouTube videos I'd been getting comparisons with Justin Bieber. But I didn't want to be the second Justin Bieber. I wanted to do something different and be the first Conor Maynard.

I was and still am a big fan of Bruno Mars, Usher, Ne-Yo and many others, but I realised very quickly that there was just no point in using other artists as references. You just have to keep working and you eventually find your own thing.

Part of the reason why the first six months of work were so unproductive was that people had a preconceived idea of what kind of music I wanted to make. I'd have a real battle when I'd go into a studio and they'd play me ideas for a really young pop song – the kind of thing that would be right for a Disney artist, but certainly not what I was into. I never really liked telling people I wasn't into their music – I was too nervous to say I didn't like it. Who was I to tell all these professional music people that I didn't like what they were doing? What had I achieved? I thought they might kick me out and then I'd be in trouble!

I did worry that things weren't going in the right direction and that maybe I'd be back at college before long, having wasted everybody's time. Despite a feeling deep down that it would all work out, there was a little bit of me wondering if I'd made a mistake.

Chapter Nine

'VEGAS GIRL'

After six months of adapting to a very new life, I got some great news from Parlophone – they were sending me out to America to write over there. New York and Los Angeles, to be exact, and this was pretty much the best news I could imagine hearing. All the artists I'd bumped into in the UK at studios while I'd been writing had talked about how amazing it was to work in America. You meet a lot of people working in the same buildings as you, so I'd chatted to Jessie J – who'd already blown up – and Rita Ora, who has the same management as me. They were really friendly, but I have to say that in those days it was a bit awkward because they had no idea who I was. I mean I wasn't anybody! I was just a kid in a studio next to the one they were in.

Jessie was actually really nice to me and posted up one of my covers on her Facebook page when we'd been chatting and I'd shown her what I did. It was 'Only Girl (In The World)' and she loved it. But I still felt like the newcomer in the company of people who were far more comfortable in that world than I was at that stage. So when Jessie talked about the writing she'd done in the States, I thought it didn't really apply to me as I hadn't earned it yet.

A three-week trip was booked and I flew to New York first to work with a few different producers and songwriters. As soon as I got there I loved it and did all the tourist stuff, going around with my camera taking pictures of Times Square and the Statue of Liberty.

Once I hit the studio I realised that just being in America had stepped up my confidence. One of the first songs I sang in the vocal booth went down really well. The producer spoke to me through the headphones and said, *'You. Are. Amazing!'* And that made my day. It was the first time I'd worked with anyone who'd said that, but I also knew that for the first time in ages I really was nailing my vocal and back on top of my game. That was more like the effect I'd had on kids in school when I'd sung in front of them, but it had kind of disappeared for a while since signing my deal, meaning I hadn't blown anyone away with my voice.

After a week of really getting a good vibe going in New York, I travelled to Los Angeles to set up in a studio with the Invisible Men. Even though we'd worked together loads in London, the idea was just to get some new space around us to be creative in.

We worked in Conway Studios, which to this day is still my favourite place to write and record. When we first walked in I was blown away. It's huge and has these amazing gardens full of trees and fantastic foliage.

My name was on the door of our studio and just down the hallway were Kiss and Lil Wayne, which made me think about the fact that *this* was where the stars came to work. Plus there was a huge kitchen full of cookies and drinks which I was allowed to help myself to! It took a while for me to realise that these things were laid on especially for me.

And it was here I wrote the first song that actually made it on to my album. It was 'Vegas Girl', which became my second single. The first thing we recorded was the chorus. I had this melody and they were feeling it, so we started talking about what kind of vibe it had to it and what the lyrics should be about. I knew it was a party kind of feeling, so I came up with the idea of a Vegas girl, because everyone knows Vegas is where you go to properly party.

That day The-Dream – an American guy who's worked with people like Britney, Rihanna, Beyoncé and just about *everyone* – was supposed to come into the session and work with us. But then he couldn't make it because he was busy, so there was just me, the Invisible Men and a writer called Scott Thomas working on the song. We made a real joke out of it, because in the end we didn't need The-Dream – we had Scott, who we called The Nightmare!

We wrote 'Vegas Girl' in just one day and played it to my manager, Sarah, who was in LA for meetings, and she loved it as well. And Miles, the head of Parlophone, went absolutely mental about it. In a good way! He was convinced it was the first single.

We also wrote 'Mary Go Round' out there, and 'Better Than You', which I did with Rita Ora. She was in LA too and since we have the same management it made sense for us to get in the studio together and see what happened.

To start with, it was a really weird vibe, because by this point Rita and I were pretty good friends so we knew we didn't want to write some lovey-dovey song, as it just wouldn't have worked. So we came up with the idea of a boy versus girl theme where each of us tries to outdo the other, inspired by that song 'Anything You Can Do, I Can Do Better'.

It was such good fun recording that song, because we were in the vocal booth together and every time Rita opened her mouth to sing I would poke her in the ribs, spoiling her take. Somewhere there's a video of us trying to out-sing each other, both doing crazy ad libs, trying to win. Obviously, being a girl, she could go so much higher, so there comes a point where I'm reaching for notes and my voice is just cracking horribly.

But Rita was so inspiring. She kept coming up with these amazing lyrics, one after the other. I reckon I went through three pizzas that day – it was my fuel of choice while recording with Rita.

That experience taught me that I work best when I'm having fun. I don't like to see songwriting as a job, but if I go in to have fun while I'm writing, I produce something so much better. I think the proof of that is the fact that one trip produced three songs which ended up on the album.

Those sessions set the tone for the rest of the album. We had finally found my sound and, I guess, found *me* as an artist. It was truly me and didn't sound like anyone else.

Just before I was due to leave, my management called me to say that Jermaine Dupri had got in touch, wanting to work with me. Initially that didn't mean anything, as he first blew up before I was really into R&B, but a quick Google search showed me what a big deal he was. He's worked with Mariah Carey, Usher, Janet Jackson and so many people, so I jumped on a plain to Atlanta to work with him.

Now this guy was cool – and he really wanted to educate me on songs from the past. He was talking to me about his breakthrough song that he wrote with two young rappers called Kris Kross – and it blew his mind when he realised that it came out the year I was born. He'd written a song for me with a sample in it from 'One In A Million' and when I said I didn't recognise it, he told me all about working with Aaliyah.

Then, when I was in the vocal booth, I was chatting to Jermaine about songs I liked and I mentioned 'Something Special' by Usher. He explained that he'd written it and that in fact the microphone I was singing into was the same one Usher had used to record that song. I actually considered kissing the mic! At that moment I guess any thought of me recording my vocals at home disappeared from my head for ever.

During my time away I made a point of staying in touch with people because otherwise it's too easy to get lost in it all. My mum phoned me seven times a day and I swapped a lot of texts with Alex – who was probably one of the most understanding friends I had. He was really cool about what I was doing and it was always exciting to tell him about how things were working out in the studio. Alex got that I was always busy and that I could only really call when I had a break, so if I didn't get back to him straight away, it wasn't like I was ignoring him.

It was the same with other friends too. I didn't want to just disappear from their lives. I wanted to keep them close and hopefully take them with me for the ride.

One of the things that had stuck with me since my meetings with Ne-Yo was that he was always surrounded by his close friends and that they were in some way connected to what he did, so they all benefited and were a part of the story.

That's how I've tried to be.

My tour manager says that me and my friends are just like that TV show *Entourage* because all of us hang out and fit into different roles. I'm the face of the squad, but everyone plays a different part, be it sorting out what club we're going to or deciding what our next move should be towards world domination!

When I left America to come home, there was a little bit of me that was kind of gutted, but it had gone so well that I knew it wouldn't be long before I was back.

I had a big upheaval to get through in the UK first, though.

Chapter Ten

LONDON CALLING

It was now September 2011 and the guys at Parlophone had really got excited about what I was doing off the back of 'Vegas Girl'.

Obviously there was still a long way to go in terms of releasing anything, but now we had a solid base to build on. What made me feel extra confident in it was that it wasn't just the label who loved it, I played it to my friends and they were really feeling it too.

Not that I could just sit about and relax now, though – my management told me it was time to move to London full-time. It was just costing too much money for me to travel up and stay in a hotel for so long and the money would go a lot further if I lived in London. I must admit I was pretty nervous about the whole idea, worrying about living on my own, having to do all my own washing, cleaning and cooking.

But even more than all that, I was pretty sure my parents wouldn't let me, even though I was eighteen and fully old enough. How wrong was I? When I broke the news to my mum, expecting tears or a point-blank refusal, she leaped up and shouted, 'Great! Do it! When are you going?'

I was gutted. Why didn't she love me any more? What had I ever done to her? Obviously I'm just kidding, and both her and my dad were really excited about my chance to move to the capital. I suppose for an eighteen-year-old from Brighton to get his own place in London is a pretty big accomplishment, so they were very proud too.

After getting over the shock of my mum wanting me out of the house (joke!), I started looking for places and soon moved into my first ever flat, in Fulham, south-west London. One of the immediate good points was that I had recently bought a pair of huge speakers which were far too loud for me to play in Brighton, but I was quite happy to turn them up now I had my own place.

My new neighbours didn't feel the same way about it, though. They hated me. It was an apartment block, so I got some serious complaints until I learned the times of day when they were out and modified my listening times.

That was fun but I didn't actually have any friends in London. Soon after I moved in, a few from Brighton started uni in London, which did make it a bit better. I would go to see them at their halls of residence or hang out with them at student bars, though that reminded me a bit of what I was missing by choosing not to go to university. The life they had was so cool and looked so fun – apart from the hard academic work, which I'm not so sad about missing.

I lived alone and they all lived together, plus they had a real social life and I didn't, which meant I relied totally on *them* for a life. They had a community around them, whereas I was going back to an empty flat and working in an industry where everyone was about twenty years older than me.

One of my closest friends – Samir, who I had been at K-BIS with – was studying at King's College, so I saw a lot more of him at least and got a taste of student life.

I guess my new lifestyle and the fact that I had a few songs in the bag led up to what was definitely the worst moment I've ever had with my label. It was my nineteenth birthday and I'd gone down to Brighton to celebrate with a big night out with my mates. I'd even flown Anth over from America to be a part of it.

I'd been so busy in the studio, seeing my friends in London and just generally doing stuff, that I had not had any time to record a new cover for YouTube and my fans in months. So Parlophone had asked me to record one and upload it – on the weekend of my birthday. I knew I was going to be partying, so I decided I'd do it a few days afterwards and put it up, no harm done.

But the day I got back to London after my party, I got a call from my management saying they were on their way to my house – which was a first. I assumed they were coming with a birthday present or just to say 'Happy birthday', but it was nothing nice. They explained that the label were really unhappy with me and wanted to know why I hadn't recorded a cover like they had asked. They were annoyed that, in fact, I hadn't even picked a song to start working on.

I realised that I had messed up and didn't have a leg to stand on. They had asked me in plenty of time and I had just not got around to it. There had been a few other things too. For example, I'd shown up late to a few writing sessions because I'd slept in after being out with my uni mates. I wasn't taking the mickey or deliberately being disrespectful, but I think I had just started to get a bit too comfortable with everything.

They told me that everyone was starting to wonder if I'd lost my drive and desire to keep working towards my goal. The label had put a lot into me – in terms of both time and money – and now I couldn't even do a single cover song when they asked me to.

At first I felt a bit annoyed, because I just hadn't seen this coming, but after sitting there thinking through it all, it hit me that I had messed up and it was my fault. I hadn't released a single song, I wasn't a star, virtually no one had heard of me and my label had spent the last year helping me find who I wanted to be as an artist.

That visit from my management really worked because I went into superdrive. I was bang on time for everything and I recorded what I think is my best ever cover video.

Anth was still in the country, staying with me, so we did 'Girls Talkin' Bout' and had a real laugh with it.

I had never wanted to upset anyone and that's a big thing for me. When people ask me what my biggest fear is, the truthful answer is that my biggest fear is disappointing people. I can't stand letting people down. A few weeks later I heard that the label were really happy with me and that Miles Leonard – the label's head – really liked the video, which was a huge relief to me.

Feeling all invigorated and with my sights set firmly back on getting more good songs recorded for my debut album, I started working in what has become my favourite London studio, Metropolis. Again, it was with the Invisible Men and, just like Conway Studios in Los Angeles, it's huge, which meant I could pace around in there. I hardly ever keep still or sit in one place for long, and when I'm writing I like to be able to move about.

Halfway through our week of recording, the Invisible Men played me this track they had been bigging up to me for a while. It was the track for the song which became 'Can't Say No'. As soon as I heard it – that really sparse but massive 'boom, boom, boom' on the intro – I knew we had to write something *sick* over it.

It was a new experience for me because we were writing in a major key over a minor-key backing track, which is what gives it that really unique vibe. It was a real challenge getting the melodies right and not just following the notes on the track.

We recorded the whole thing in a day and I remember listening back that evening and doing the Dougie to it and loving it. That dance is like my little celebration dance. Which is actually the worst feeling you can have, because it's immediately followed by the horrible thought, what if the label don't like it?

We went in to the label and played it to Miles and I would have been really wounded if he hadn't been into it. But he loved it straight away and said it should be the set-up single. A set-up single is the first song an artist releases and isn't really aimed at the charts. It's more about trying to get a few radio plays and getting your name and sound out there.

So we now had my set-up single, my second single – 'Vegas Girl' – and quite a few tracks that were looking good for the album.

I announced to my fans that I would soon be releasing an album and they went mental, so I decided to start doing video diaries – or blogs – right up until when I released it.

As a joke I was going to call my blog Conor's Daynard, but I put it out to the fans to decide what I should go for and the poll came back with the name the Conorcles. It was a good way of staying in touch with all those people who had been loyal to me and showing them what I was doing.

Then came the bad news – well, it worried me a bit anyway – that the label wanted me to put on a showcase for everyone involved in the project. Now you have to remember I'd only ever sung live in front of people at school at this stage and not one person from my management or my label had actually seen me on a stage.

I was bricking it! I was *so* nervous. But it did mean I got a band together for the first time too, which was great. There have been a few line-up changes since then, but my drummer, Tonez, has been there from the start and he's my boy.

It was strange practising all my songs with the band, because it was doing live-instrument versions of tracks which had been written with synths in the studio, so the sound was very different.

I had no idea what to do onstage, so I had a couple of choreographers teach me how to move around a bit and just perform a little more.

After a little while I began to relax and just thought to myself, I know I can sing, so when the day comes and I'm in front of everyone from the label, I'll just go for it.

I remember watching them all filter into the rehearsal room, then the lights dimmed and I went up on to this small stage. I was absolutely dying inside but when I finished what felt like the longest time I had ever been on a stage in my life, I looked up and they were all clapping and looking really impressed.

This was a *huge* milestone as it was the first time I had ever performed to anyone publicly who wasn't a friend, family member or at school.

I'm really glad the news I was given when I came offstage had been kept from me until *after* I'd sung. Because I'd probably have needed to perform the whole set sitting down if I'd found out beforehand.

Chapter Eleven

COMPLETING MY ALBUM

I looked around the rehearsal room and saw Miles and Elias deep in conversation, but the moment I caught Miles's eye he beckoned me down from the stage to talk to them. With my heart in my mouth, I made my way over, wondering what the full verdict would be as they both looked very serious.

'We've got an issue,' said Miles. 'What do you think, Conor?'

I had no idea what he was talking about, but it didn't sound good. 'Haven't you told him?' he asked Elias.

Elias shook his head. 'I thought you'd told him. Shall we tell him?'

This went on for about twenty seconds as I got more and more worried and wound up, before Elias eventually said, 'You're going to Miami to work with Pharrell Williams.'

It was like a moment out of a dream. If I'd been given the chance to pick just one producer I would like to work with, I would have said Pharrell. It turned out he had called the label to find out about working with me, as he had seen my YouTube videos and he'd heard a rumour that Parlophone had signed me. Even now I can't believe that he actually sought me out. I can't emphasise enough that, as far as I am concerned, Pharrell is pretty much the most talented guy on the planet.

Funnily enough, he'd actually called hoping that I *hadn't* signed my deal yet as he was hoping to sign me himself. Luckily for me, he wanted to work with me anyway. This meant I was going to one of the most amazing places in the world and that I would be working with a guy who'd produced and written with Justin Timberlake and had been a part of the Neptunes and N.E.R.D.

The plan was to send me out to Miami in January – in just over a month's time – when I'd finished up a few things in the UK studio. Obviously I was excited and kept checking over the next few weeks for a specific date in January to look forward to. And then it got pushed all the way back to March. How I got through those months without pulling all my hair out I do not know!

But eventually the time came and I jumped on a plane out to Miami to meet the legend.

I couldn't have had a much worse start, though. On the day I was to start work in Pharrell's studio I had the most terrible food poisoning I'd ever experienced. I struggled in to the studio, but ten minutes before he arrived I was still throwing up. And I'm talking about projectile vomiting here. I could have hit a wall ten feet away.

But I knew there was no way I could call off the session. I had to pull through it. I remember being terrified that if I met Pharrell and threw up in front of him, I'd die of shame and never live it down. Luckily I'd managed to get most of it out by the time he got there and he was cool about me not feeling 100 per cent.

The main thing was, I quickly realised he's just a really nice guy. I asked him how he'd heard about me and he told me he'd seen my cover of Justin Timberlake's 'Senorita' a few years back. He'd been following my covers ever since then. He even told me he'd left messages for me on my YouTube account – which I just hadn't seen because they'd got lost with all the others in there.

To be honest, even if I'd seen them I wouldn't have believed they were really from him. The idea that he was watching me when I was just sitting in my bedroom in Hove recording covers is so surreal.

After we'd chatted a bit he said something really weird. 'I want you to be a band.'

Er, oh dear, Pharrell's not making sense here.

But when he broke it down, I got his point. He wanted me to go for a kind of Maroon 5 vibe with a band, but the whole thing should still just be called Conor Maynard. His argument was that as a solo singer I would always be compared to, or competing with, Justin Bieber, Justin Timberlake and all those other solo stars.

The thing is, it was too late to start changing my style, as I'd been working on my album for a while, we had some great tracks and my history was as a solo singer anyway.

But I have to say, working with Pharrell was the weirdest experience. He writes totally by himself. He'll sit there for half an hour and make a track that he really likes the sound of, put that track on his iPod, go outside and ride his skateboard while he writes the entire song in his head. Then he comes back into the studio and lays down a guide vocal of the song he's just written.

I then go into the booth to record my bits and ideas with the engineer overseeing everything, while Pharrell plays Mario Kart on the Wii and chips in over his shoulder.

The week I spent in Miami with Pharrell was the one in which I met the most stars in my life. On my third day in the studio I was just about to nip out when the door opened and almost hit me in the face. Standing right in front of me was Ludacris.

Every time anyone came into the studio, Pharrell made a point of playing what we had been working on to the newcomer. So he introduced me to Ludacris and played him what we had been working on. I can't explain how unreal it felt watching Ludacris with his eyes shut, nodding his head as my voice blasted over the speakers.

A few days later a guy called Tyler, The Creator turned up – and he is one of Pharrell's best mates as well as a hugely creative artist, which meant he was happily telling Pharrell all about what he should and shouldn't be doing.

So Tyler was chatting away to Pharrell and not that bothered about me being there, plus he had about six of his crew with him, while I sat there quietly feeling a bit out of place.

Then I heard Pharrell saying he wanted to play some of the music we'd been working on and I was thinking, please don't – this guy's gonna hate it!

Tyler's a really hip hop guy and obviously his vibe was so different from what I do. Anyway, Pharrell played some of our bits and pieces and the feeling in the room changed so much. Tyler got all animated and started bouncing about and talking to me for the first time.

He said, '*Shiiiiit!* You sound like a young Michael Jackson in his *Off The Wall* era.'

Talk about an unexpected compliment.

Tyler obviously hadn't been expecting much from me – I guess because of the way I looked.

Eventually two tracks made it on to my album, 'Glass Girl' and 'Lift Off', which both sound so cool with that unique Pharrell vibe. Working with him was an honour. On the very last day of my trip over to Miami, Pharrell told me he wanted to take me to a Tyler, The Creator concert as a goodbye present.

We ended up standing actually on the stage at the side and I had to pinch myself because on one side of me was Pharrell and on the other was Lil Wayne, with all three of us nodding away to the song. I felt like, 'Yeah, this is how I roll!'

The next day I jumped on a plane to Los Angeles as we'd managed to sneak in a recording session with Ne-Yo as a part of the trip.

I had a backing track from Stargate – these amazing producers – which I was really feeling and I wanted Ne-Yo to try to write something over it for me. He came up with an idea which, when he played it to me, I knew straight away was massive. I went straight in to record it and I loved it *so* much. It was 'Turn Around'.

But when we sat there listening to it together, Ne-Yo was smiling and I could see him mulling something over in his head. I had a sinking feeling in the pit of my stomach. I knew he was going to take it for himself and release it as his own single, even though he had written it for me.

He said, 'I think ... I should be on this song with you.' That blew my mind. Inside I was screaming, *'Yesss!!!'* like a little girl at the thought that I was going to duet with Ne-Yo, and willing him to go and record it right then so he couldn't change his mind. But I knew I had to act a bit cool, so what I actually said was, 'Yeah, man, that would be a cool thing to think about.'

Obviously I went for it and when his vocals were on the track it sounded massive.

So there it was. In a little over a year of writing and working with some of the most amazing producers anywhere, I had my debut album pretty much ready to go. I'd worked with the Invisible Men, Ne-Yo, Pharrell Williams and Rita Ora, to name just a few, and I'd even been given a song by Frank Ocean called 'Pictures', which I loved as well.

But there was still one major problem. I hadn't managed to get my original partner in music, Anth, on a single song. Ever since I'd got signed, I'd made it clear to my label that I wanted to keep him a part of it. Parlophone had flown him over really early on for some of my writing sessions in late 2010 and that was how we'd finally first met face to face.

I picked Anth up from the airport and he stayed with me at my parents' house for about a month. It was weird when we first met, because we knew each other so well, but the friendship was real and worked even better when we got together.

We had the same sense of humour and we really enjoyed our time together in the studio, even though none of the songs we had worked on quite worked out.

Now it was almost time to wrap up the album and we still had no songs with Anth on. But my label agreed with me that as he had been a part of my whole musical process, it was essential that he feature on the album.

However, one day well into 2012 I found myself sitting in a meeting with my label, talking about the tracklisting for the album – which songs were going on and in what order – when I suddenly realised this was it. It was almost too late to get Anth on the album. Elias went pale and said, 'Oh my God ... he *has* to be on it.' So in the end what we did was send him 'Headphones' and he threw a verse on it.

We did it just in time to make sure it got on as the bonus track on the iTunes album, which was such a relief as my debut album without Anth would have just been wrong.

It was necessary for me, him and all the fans who had supported me from the start.

For me, that meant I had finished the album, done everything and it had everyone I wanted on it.

Chapter Twelve

MTV BRAND NEW FOR 2012

At the end of 2011 I was in the Parlophone office for a meeting with Elias, who told me that MTV were really feeling my music. We'd played a few of my tracks to some key people at MTV radio and TV, just to gauge how they felt about the project. As a result, I was going to be a part of their Brand New For 2012.

Every year MTV pick nine signed artists and one unsigned artist out of all the new artists put forward and then throw it open to a public vote. Even getting on to that list out of the potential thousands of people going in for it was a real privilege. And when I saw the list of names I was up against my heart fell – it was some tough competition for a young lad from Hove! Lana Del Rey, Delilah, Angel and Michael Kiwanuka, for a start. I totally accepted that I wasn't going to win, but I thought I would at least give it a good go and enjoy it all.

So all our names were put up on MTV's site and whoever got the most votes got priority rotations, which basically means your single and video get played all the time and they give you amazing exposure for the entire year.

That's massive, especially for a new artist as MTV is the go-to channel for music.

For me, this was pretty much the moment where I went from being a kid doing stuff in the studio that no one had ever heard of, to being in the public eye.

I began doing interviews with people, starting with an interview for MTV at their Brand New event – and I needed a makeover before I went there. I got a haircut and some new clothes because I had to step up and behave like a real artist now. I couldn't just show up to everything in jogging bottoms. I'd met a stylist called Cobbie Yates who I really got on with and to this day he's responsible for making sure I look the part.

Wretch 32 had won the year before, and now I was there with most of the other people on the list to talk about who we were and what we would do if we ever made it big. It felt really

weird being asked questions in front of a camera for the first time and I realised that I'd have to learn to think on my feet, otherwise it would be too easy to end up saying either nothing at all or something incredibly stupid!

They asked me if I'd like to do anything for charity and I said, 'Er, I'd love to do things for charity,' but my mind went totally blank and I couldn't think of any of the charities that were important to me.

I learned a lot from that interview. I needed to teach myself how to do that part of my job.

It's been a real learning curve over the last year and a half, understanding just how people can get the wrong impression of you from the way you behave or carry yourself in an interview.

Record labels do research on their artists and ask perhaps 100 members of the public for their opinions on an act and their music. And the early results were awful for me to hear. The general feeling was that I was arrogant and had done nothing to deserve success. It really stung me.

I learned that people don't know your story unless you tell them. They had just assumed that because I was young I had been plucked out of nowhere and taught to behave a certain way. That really hurt me, because I hate arrogant people and artists who think they are better than others, just because they have a career in music.

Wherever I am, I always try to treat everyone equally. If I'm at a radio station, I don't talk down to the work experience people, and I'm as nice to them as I am to the head of the station or the top DJ.

It felt so bad because arrogant was exactly the opposite of what I was. I can only assume they thought I was that way because I became confident in front of the camera and was a bit cheeky in interviews. So I've learned that I need to make a point of telling people how I earned my stripes on YouTube and to make sure I'm less OTT in interviews.

Still, that day at MTV was like a little taste of what my life as an artist was going to be about, with red carpets, cameras and reporters.

But when the event was finished, the real support from my fans kicked in and this was the first time I found out just how loyal so many of those people who'd watched my YouTube videos truly were.

Fans had to go on to the MTV website and vote for their favourite artist in the Top Ten over the course of a couple of months. Whoever got the most votes won MTV Brand New For 2012.

The thing is, I hadn't realised that voting had already opened, so when I logged on to the website for my first look, I was eighth on the list. I knew even as I looked at it that there was no way I was going to win this. But I tweeted to my fans anyway, hoping that they'd vote for me and maybe move me up a space or two on the list.

Within an hour I was at Number One – which was unbelievable. Lana Del Rey was at Number Ten, so I thought that, even though she would surely win, it would take a while for her to climb up to the top and knock me off.

In my head I had kind of decided that everyone who was going to vote for me had already done it, so there was no way I was going to hang on to that position.

One day Lana jumped from tenth place to second and I realised that her fans had finally worked out that they needed to come and vote for her on MTV's website.

That was it.

She was coming for me and I wouldn't win. How could I compete against the mighty Lana? There was no way of checking figures or anything, so the last week before results were announced was horrible and my mum checked every day to see if I was still at Number One.

Then the call came. MTV were on the phone and they told me I'd won! It just didn't make sense. I didn't understand how I could have held on against Lana and the others.

But it was fan power. My fans truly are the most loyal out there because not only had I won, but I had got as many votes as all the other nine artists in the competition put together.

I couldn't tell anyone officially for a few days, but my brother was up to visit me in London and when I told him I'd won he went mad and jumped on me, shouting, 'Yesss!!!'

When I tweeted the news the following week, my fans went mad – I wanted to respond to every one of them who had voted, but I would never have got it done, so I just wrote, 'Mayniacs Go HARD!'

I do love my Mayniacs. The name first came about when I decided I needed one for my fans. Jessie J had her Heartbeats and I wanted something too. I tweeted asking my fans to think of ideas and two main names kept coming up. One was the Mayniacs and the other was the Condoms! There was just no way I could see myself walking out onstage and saying, 'What's happening, Condoms?' I'd have got arrested!

There was a slight glitch with the MTV win, though. The 'Can't Say No' video – which was my set-up single, remember – wasn't ready in time for MTV to show it so I had to use a very quick and rough video that I had made originally just for YouTube. Basically, me and a cameraman had walked around London and gone on the tube just shooting me randomly singing bits of the song.

MTV were absolutely brilliant. There's no doubt they played a massive part in boosting my profile and my career over that whole year and right up until the present day. They were on board so early and were so positive with everything that I did and I am so grateful.

As a result of winning that contest, I got to go to the Brits shortly afterwards and walk along the red carpet, with virtually no one showing any interest in me because I hadn't released a song and never been on the radio! I got to the end of the carpet and MTV were there and they were the only people to talk to me.

Obviously things have changed a lot since then, but MTV paved the way for me to develop as an artist who became bigger than just YouTube and the internet, and they were my first step into the world of mainstream music.

The circle was complete in early 2013 when I went back to perform at the MTV Brand New For 2013 event, which was won – as I said before – by Ebony Day, the girl I'd once duetted with on YouTube.

God, it's a small world!

Chapter Thirteen

MY FIRST SINGLE

It's February 2012 – a month or so before I go out to Miami to work with Pharrell – and I've just won MTV's Brand New For 2012. My album is close to complete and, after loads of meetings and conversations between me, my management and Parlophone, we've decided that 'Can't Say No' is going to be my set-up single – a kind of a test single to gauge people's reactions.

We weren't expecting too much in terms of chart positions with the song because it was the first time I had ever released anything and – other than the amazing 'Mayniacs' I already had – there wasn't a huge market of people out there waiting to hear from me. Maybe 50,000 people were following me on Facebook and Twitter.

I was just happy 'Cant Say No' was getting released because it had always been the song I'd wanted to come out first since the day I'd recorded it.

Remember how in the last chapter I told you I didn't have the video for the song ready in time for MTV to play it? Well, I actually had shot a full video in December 2011. It was absolutely amazing too. I had to go into rehearsals with all these incredibly hot girl dancers, which was really annoying because none of them had heard of me!

I had to really concentrate to be able to sing and dance in front of them.

It was all shot in black and white and looked really deep, serious and mature, and was almost abstract, with shots of me in silhouette with a picture frame around me.

A few weeks after we shot it, my manager told me there was a bit of a problem – no one at the label liked the video. I was gutted. I hadn't even seen the finished video yet and I had no real idea of what this meant. I didn't know if I looked really bad, or if I'd somehow messed it up or if the whole thing had just come out rubbish.

Was I going to record a new video or had they decided at the last minute that in fact none of this would work and that was it for me? I thought I might be heading back to Brighton as a failed pop star, hoping to finish my final year at school and then find a university that would take me.

'I'm sorry to tell you this, Conor,' said my manager, 'you're going to have to shoot a new video.'

Phew. Why he hadn't told me that first, I'll never know. For a few moments the bottom had dropped out of my world. The label felt that although it was a good video, it just wasn't right for me as an artist. I wasn't convinced, but when they showed me it I understood. It did look cool, but it was also too serious, given the song is so young and tongue in cheek.

To this day no one has ever seen that video.

So we came up with a brand-new video and I knew we had to nail this as there would be no third shot at getting it right. I made it with a young Urban director called Rohan Blair-Mangat and we went for the idea of a cool house party, a bit like an Adidas advert.

We shot the video at this house in east London and I got my brother to be in it as one of the partygoers. There were so many hot girls again that none of us knew where to look! This video just felt right as we were making it and it fitted the song – really good fun, tongue in cheek and a bit silly.

I mean, I'm obviously not serious in those lyrics about girls, girls, girls. Wherever I go I'm obviously not *really* covered in girls! I do get attention in clubs or if I'm at a show, but I can go out without being mobbed by girls ripping my clothes off.

Everyone was a lot more happy with this video when it was finished and I cannot tell you how good that made me feel. I wanted the video for my first ever song to be something that we all 100 per cent believed in.

But, just as I was enjoying the feeling of things coming together, with the MTV win and the video looking great, something happened that threw a shadow over everything. Radio 1 didn't like the song and said they wouldn't play it. It was a real body blow.

Whenever you release a song, it goes to radio weeks before it actually comes out, but if they don't play it it's an immense problem for any artist, especially a new one who is trying to gain support. And Radio 1 is the *big* hitter, the one you need on your team to get the song out there to everyone in the UK.

They had heard a couple of my songs and the feedback hadn't been good. They weren't sure they were feeling 'Vegas Girl' – my follow-up single – either, although they did like 'Pictures'. That was good to hear at least, but there had never been any plans for 'Pictures' to be a single and it just wasn't the right song to come out with first. It was something we'd have to work our way up to, as it was too mature a song for a young artist like me to come out with. It wouldn't have made sense to start with that and follow up with a party song like 'Vegas Girl'.

I went home and phoned Anth to tell him the news and basically say, 'It's going to flop.' That's how negative I was feeling.

Without radio play you're relying on a miracle to break a song. You need an online phenomenon that just blows up on its own, like Gotye's 'Somebody That I Used To Know' did. There's maybe one a year that does that.

Regardless of this, I started on the promotional work, doing radio interviews with lots of people, including Radio 1! It felt odd doing little chats with them, when I knew they weren't even playing my song.

But then the news came through that Radio 1Xtra had put it straight on their C list, which meant they would give it some support. Obviously the A list is best, but just being on 1Xtra is a very cool way to start off. The song started climbing because people were feeling it, so they moved it up on to the B list and then eventually the A list, which meant they really were getting behind it hard. Maybe things were going to be OK after all.

One of the things we needed to impress Radio 1 was good viewing numbers on the 'Can't Say No' video. After all, if lots of people are watching, then it means those same people will probably want to hear it on the radio too.

The video was due to go up on a Friday and in the few days beforehand I had been preparing my Twitter followers by saying I wanted to get something trending around the video release. I was sure I didn't have the fan power to manage that, but I had to try.

On the Friday I tweeted the Mayniacs to start trying to get it trending just before I went into the studio with the Invisible Men. By the time I had got down the stairs and into the studio – less than a minute – it was trending Number One worldwide on Twitter. It was such a proud moment for me and my fans, because it was all about them. *They* made that happen for me.

Over the weekend I think it had got about 150,000 views, which was good, but it wasn't massive, and on Monday the label got in touch and said they really wanted it to be up to a million views by the end of the week. Yeah, right. As if that's going to happen. That made it hard for me for the rest of the day because I was doing magazine interviews and I just had in the back of my mind that I was going to disappoint my label, after all that hard work.

I checked the views daily and it started to jump up, by several hundred thousand views a day, until it eventually did hit the million mark by the end of the week. It was amazing – the song was blowing up.

That's where I was when I got a call telling me 'Can't Say No' had been put on to the C list at Radio 1. I remember doing a jumping high five because we were so happy about it – especially as I'd had to win them over and earn it.

And then – just like the video had on YouTube – the song started to grow. Taking on a life of its own, 'Can't Say No' worked its way up to the Radio 1 A list and I had incredible support from everyone there, not to mention Capital and Kiss and everyone else. It even became one of Capital's anthems.

The thing with Radio 1 was that once I started actually doing interviews with them, they realised that I'm not just some manufactured product who's been given everything. They could see that I had done all my own work via YouTube and earned my right to be an artist.

Then the pre-orders started to come in, meaning we could have a look at what kind of sales we might be able to expect. The numbers were surprising. Remember this was just my set-up single, so we weren't expecting anything saleswise. Yet the figures were matching songs that were getting into the Top Five in the charts. This was ridiculous! It was looking like my set-up single was in fact going to be my *first* single! Much more than just an early calling card, 'Can't Say No' was actually going to chart.

In the week of release, in early April, the song sold 85,000 copies – which was unbelievable. In any other week that would have been more than enough to go all the way to Number One, but it just so happened that Carly Rae Jepsen released 'Call Me Maybe' the week before and kept me off the top by selling well over 100,000 copies.

None of us had been expecting anything even close to the sales I'd got, despite the radio support and the views on the video. No one has any right to expect that kind of chart performance from a brand-new artist releasing their debut single.

I'd come so close to Number One, but having a first single getting to the second spot actually suited me. I didn't really want the first song I released hitting the top, because then the only way you can go from that is down, unless you get Number One after Number One. And I wanted some space to grow.

Chapter Fourteen

'CONTRAST' TOPS THE CHARTS

With the 'Can't Say No' video getting well over a million views and a Number Two chart placing for my debut release, I have a strong memory of my manager saying to me, 'Are you ready not to be able to walk around the streets any more?' I asked him what he meant and he said, 'This is it. This is the moment. You're going to be famous.'

It was really weird because I'd turn up at Capital or Radio 1 for an interview and there would be fans waiting there outside for me, shouting my name for the first time ever. Then it moved on to happening on the street. Now that was *really* strange. When that first started I really didn't know how to handle it. Walking to the Underground one day in Fulham shortly after the song had come out, I was stopped about ten times. I called my manager and said, 'Er, you were right – I don't think I'm going to be able to take the train any more!'

That's because I would and still do stop for everyone who says hi to me. It was mainly young girls asking for a picture and some of them would actually freak out a little bit, which felt weird for me because of course I was still just Conor. I don't think you ever think of yourself as a celebrity, or a big deal, even when other people see you that way.

The darker side of it was when people found out where I lived in Fulham and started waiting outside my house.

People had started watching me walk home and one day when I'd nipped out to Sainsbury's I came back to find someone had posted a note through my letter box with their number asking me to call them.

Eventually I had to move out because some of the older kids in the area started to get a bit funny. One day I came home and there were about ten guys just hanging about outside my place and the woman who owns the pub opposite told me they'd been trying to take pictures through my letter box.

Those moments were a bit scary. Being stopped by teenage girls is fun, but groups of guys checking out your house when you are out is less enjoyable!

It sounds weird, but I suppose I was becoming more famous and recognisable and with that, I gained more fans. My Twitter followers increased too so that soon I had 400,000 people looking at my tweets – and that number kept growing until today I have over 1.4 million!

Now I can literally trend whatever I want at any second, so I am very careful about what I tweet because that is a lot of responsibility to have. I definitely don't go on Twitter if I've had a couple of drinks, to make sure I don't say anything I might regret. It's got to the point where if I meet someone I get on with and start following them, thousands of my followers will then go and immediately start following them off the back of it. My brother's got about 44,000 followers and most of them are Mayniacs. My best friend, Alex, has just over 14,000.

Sometimes I get people that I've never really been close with asking me for things or acting as if we've been friends in the past. There were these two kids from Brighton who would call me every day, saying they wanted to hang out with me in London or whatever. One of them I hadn't even been friends with in Brighton – we'd just got the same bus!

I came to realise that I had to be careful not to believe all the people who were willing to suck up to me just to party or hang out. It got to the stage where so many people had passed my number around that I would have to give my phone to a friend to answer, to stop me speaking to some random who was pestering me.

And I started to get nasty comments as well, particularly after I'd been on big TV shows like *Celebrity Juice*, *Alan Carr: Chatty Man* and *The Graham Norton Show*. I understood that people had their views, but then I got tweets telling me I should kill myself, or that I was the ugliest thing that had ever been born into this world. At first it was horrible to read and I didn't understand why I was getting this abuse. I think I responded once, but that's what they want and I learned just to ignore it. I had to tell myself to focus on the positives, and I try to tell myself that one day all those haters will get it and then we'll be cool. It does still get to me, though, I must admit.

But life was good in general and I also got on the road gigging, doing three tours in 2012. I had a band around me who I loved and our first tour was pretty small, doing academies around the country. We had a splitter bus that we travelled in, which I loved. It's split into three sections, with the driver at the front, then the area where the band sit and at the back a section to carry all the equipment from show to show. You don't sleep in it, you just hit the road and then stay in hotels.

My first ever gig was in Brighton at a place called the Haunt, in front of all my friends, and I knew *everyone* in the place. It was when 'Can't Say No' had only just gone on the radio. I was awful – I honestly didn't let go of the microphone stand even once because I was so nervous for the entire half-hour set. What always made me most nervous was interacting. I knew I could do the songs, but what the hell do you say to the audience in between them?

I threw a few covers in to keep people happy, but of course they'd never heard any of my songs before and so they couldn't sing along to them. Apart from 'Can't Say No', that is – I couldn't believe it when I started singing and everyone in the place knew it and joined in on the chorus.

I had a similar moment at the end of March when I'd been getting some good radio play and I performed at the Girl Guides Big Gig, where me and Rita Ora were two of the newcomers. There were some big names there, including Olly Murs and the Saturdays. I remember I looked at all those big stars, thinking to myself, I'm going to go out there onstage and no one's going to know who I am!

I was only there to sing 'Can't Say No', so I thought at least the pain of singing to thousands of people all wondering who the hell the kid onstage was wouldn't last long.

When they announced 'Conor Maynard' before I walked onstage, the place exploded. I'd never heard so much noise in my life and it was the very opposite of what I had been expecting. The audience were all singing along and screaming my name and it was the very first time I had ever truly experienced that on such a big scale with people I had never seen before.

One of the dates that I did was on the day that 'Can't Say No' went into the charts at Number Two, and when we announced it onstage the crowd went mental. But that tour and the second one were mainly just to get me used to gigging and we deliberately kept them quite intimate.

There were exceptions of course – like the Capital Summertime Ball in June – which was at Wembley Stadium in front of 80,000 people, with me again singing just 'Can't Say No'. It went off again. Everyone knew the song and I buzzed so much off their vibe. There was a runway leading down from the stage into the crowd and I didn't waste a second. I just ran straight down it and did the whole song from the middle of the crowd. I absolutely loved it.

Being in the studio and performing live are my two favourite things, but they are so different. One is fun and intimate; the other is feeding back off the audience and actually being a part of an interactive music experience with your fans.

With momentum now really building and some good shows under my belt, plus the success of the single still fresh, it was important that we push on and keep things going, as our plan was to release the album a week after the second single came out.

We set up a tour for July to coincide with the release of 'Vegas Girl' and got going on the video ahead of the release date. We had to really think about how to shoot that video. The obvious choice was to shoot it in Las Vegas in a casino. But the problem was that I wouldn't have been allowed in any of the casinos as I was only nineteen! So we had to think of a clever way around it.

We came up with the idea that the 'Vegas Girl' is actually just a girl wearing a T-shirt with those two words on it. I bump into her on the street at the start and then spend the rest of the video trying to track her down to get her to come to my party. It was a really cool idea but there's an incredibly awkward talking sequence at the very beginning that makes me cringe every time I watch it, it's so horrible.

When we meet I say something about wanting to give her a massage and then ask for her number, and with my terrible chat-up lines I come across as really sleazy! In fact the conversation was way longer and made sense in a jokey way, but they edited it down until I looked like such a creep, basically offering to rub her! That was the bit that all my mates ripped into me for when they saw it and I still haven't lived it down.

But the rest of the video was absolutely sick. We shot it in New York on the top of a building called 5 Pointz, which was just covered in amazing graffiti and had amazing views of the city from the roof.

The main girl in the video is this smoking hot – and lovely – model called Allura Dana. During the shoot we really got on and became very close. I didn't get tired of looking at her, I have to say!

There was great support again, including from Vevo Lift, who pick a new artist and really promote their videos and music. I got that from MTV as well, so the 'Vegas Girl' video was absolutely rinsed all over the TV as well as radio, which was a really big boost for me.

But one thing that we had all forgotten was that summer 2012 was all about one thing – the Olympics. The Games in London started on Friday, 27 July and my album was due to come out on Monday the 30th. Talk about bad timing for me! It meant I would be battling with the biggest event the UK had seen in years to try to get people to pay attention not only to my new single, but also to my debut album.

'Vegas Girl' went in at Number Four, which was another amazing feeling as that meant two hit singles out of two, although what was really on my mind was the album, due out just seven days later. I loved that people loved 'Vegas Girl' as much as I did and I knew it was worthy of being a Top Five track, but it was just one song out of a whole collection I was proud of.

Naming the album took a while because I couldn't decide what to stick with and I didn't actually settle on the title until about a month before it was due for release. The first idea was 'I Think We've Got A Problem', as a kind of cocky but tongue-in-cheek touch. As well as being from the lyrics of 'Can't Say No', it was basically saying what all other artists out there would be saying once they heard how amazing my album was! But I was never really comfortable with it because I knew that in trying to explain that title, it would always come over as arrogant even though it was meant as a joke.

I was talking about it with one of the Invisible Men and he said I should call my second album *Contrast*, because it was a great way of suggesting that I had grown and changed. I loved the title straight away but I knew that was what I wanted to call my *first* album. It just made sense to me because it fitted in so many ways.

First, there was the contrast between what everyone was expecting and what the album actually was. It wasn't the Bieber 2.0 album they were anticipating. Then there was the contrast between all the songs on it, from party anthems to stripped-back ballads and vibes. And finally the contrast between what I looked like and the way I sounded.

When *Contrast* was released I genuinely didn't have any expectations. I just wanted it to do as well as it possibly could and, if anything, I was nervous that if it wasn't well received, I'd feel like I'd let down all those people who had been a part of it with me. I was totally proud of the album and I wanted as many people as possible to hear it.

To promote it, I did a few signings up and down the country and not only was everyone talking about the Olympics, but I had a battle on my hands with Plan B, who had released his album *Ill Manors* the week before and was sitting at the top of the album charts.

Then, really early on the Sunday morning, I got a call from my label to tell me that *Contrast* had gone in at Number One. Now this will sound really strange, but the first thing I did when I put the phone down was go straight back to sleep. As well as being a very early call, it was almost too much for me to deal with, and I kind of shut down so I could process it all when I woke up. And when I did that, it all sank in and I was over the moon.

Even now, for me, *Contrast* going to Number One is the biggest and best thing that has ever happened to me. That day, to celebrate, I went to see a film and I remember sitting there thinking to myself, I wonder if anyone here realises that they are sitting in the same cinema as the person who has got the best-selling album in the whole country!

That was an odd but amazing feeling, a hand-on-heart feeling. I was so chuffed with myself. It mattered so much more to me than having a Number One single, because an album is your body of work, it's you. A single is just a little representation, but your album means everything and I felt like my fans had put *me* at Number One.

And it wasn't just the UK. *Contrast* went Top Ten in Canada and did really well in Europe too. Later in the year they even gave me an award in Belgium!

That night I went out and there were so many paparazzi outside the club we were in, Whisky Mist, taking pictures of me and all my mates, who had come up from Brighton to help me celebrate. And Anth had sent me the longest essay ever on email, congratulating me, so I was feeling on top of the world.

Chapter Fifteen

'TURN AROUND' AND TAKING ON AMERICA

That feeling of euphoria lasted a long time – mainly because cool things kept happening.

Off the back of that Number One and 'Vegas Girl' getting played everywhere, I got booked to play V Festival in August in their Undercover Tent, which was for emerging artists.

But unfortunately when I peered into the tent half an hour before I was due to go on, there were just ten people milling about looking at the stage. I was properly cacking it, thinking I would end up performing to a handful of bored festivalgoers. Things didn't look too good for me, which meant I was in the worst mood.

My drummer, Tonez, took me to one side and said, 'Mate, they will come. People know who you are and they will come to listen to you.' I wasn't so sure. At other shows there had just been one stage, so everyone there had kind of had to watch me. But this was a festival with loads of tents and big names headlining on other stages, so people would actually have to choose to come and see me rather than someone else.

By the time I walked on to the stage – having prepared myself for the worst – I was amazed to see the whole of that massive tent packed out. That was one of my favourite gigs ever, because it just wasn't what I was expecting, and the set went down a storm.

Not long afterwards it was time to shoot the video for the Ne-Yo single, 'Turn Around', so I flew out to Los Angeles and made what is 100 per cent the most fun video I have made in my life. Even more fun than 'Vegas Girl'. Just for me they shut off a whole block in downtown LA, sprayed the location with water and started filming! There's me dancing, me messing around with Ne-Yo, and both of us posing and playing up for the camera. And without being too crude about it, we spent *a lot* of money on that video, making it the most expensive one I've been in.

The director we used was Colin Tilley, who is the sickest young videomaker out there. He's only about twenty-five, but he's made videos for Chris Brown, Justin Timberlake, Nicki Minaj,

50 Cent and basically everyone who is a big name. Colin is one of my favourite directors of all time. He was properly into me as an artist too, which made the video really fun to shoot.

One thing I want to clear up is the scene where I'm in a telephone box suspended eighty feet up in the air. Everyone to this day thinks that's fake, or filmed on a green screen or something, but I swear it's not! I really was in that little box hanging off a crane for hours on end above an aqueduct.

On the plus side I was in there with this fire-hot girl called Britt Karolina, who was six years older than me and just about the most beautiful woman I have ever laid eyes on. It was heaven. And I was scoffing chewing gum constantly to make sure I smelt fresh!

It was a bit scary up there, but obviously I had to try to act manly in front of Britt, although I did tell her that if we went down I would be climbing on top of her to save myself. What a gent, eh?

Then for the next scene we both had to stand on top of a moving bus, which is as dangerous as it sounds, I can tell you. We had our ankles chained to the sides of the bus so that if we fell we wouldn't die, we would just be left hanging with our ankles or something broken!

The bus was only moving at about five miles an hour, but when you are standing on top of it trying to look cool, mime your song and dance at the same time, trust me, it feels a lot faster and keeping your balance is difficult.

At the end of the shoot, before he left, Ne-Yo came over and said, 'I'll see you at the VMAs next year!' I felt like I'd just arrived in the big time!

The thing with this third single was that it was a track on the album and so people had the song already. Plus when people heard it on the radio, they could just go and buy the song then and there – there was no specific release date. Songs like that never chart very high, because people buy them over a longer period of time, rather than rushing out in the same week to get a newly released song. That means it's possible to sell more singles than lots of other people over a period of time but not make the Top Five.

In the end, 'Turn Around' stayed in the charts for fourteen weeks. It *flew* and I think it was the most successful of all my singles even though it peaked at Number Eight.

By the end of 2012 I'd sold a million singles in total – which is more than I'd ever dreamed of. The funny thing is, I didn't know that until the day I was performing at the Capital Jingle Bell Ball at the end of the year when the announcer said my name during the soundcheck and then added, 'He's sold an amazing one million singles.' I told my manager about the mistake so that it could be changed before the show, but it turned out it was true!

previous page
My dressing room while on tour with Ne-Yo

At the end of October and in early November I did my first big UK headline tour – this was the album tour. My band was made up of Drew Campbell on bass, Emlyn Maillard on keys, Tonez on drums and Ross Chapman on guitar.

I'd flown Anth over for the tour and he performed 'Headphones' with me towards the end of my set, which sent the fans absolutely mental because they weren't expecting him. We also did a version of Jay Z's 'Public Service Announcement' and I rapped it while he was doing loads of ad libs. It was so much fun. Plus I had my mate from Brighton, George Leighton – aka G23 – as tour DJ, so I had a proper little crew of friends with me.

I headlined at Shepherd's Bush Empire, which totally sold out. That was an amazing experience because so many massive artists play this venue, which, although it's big, still has a really intimate vibe to it.

The weirdest show of them all was in my hometown, at the Brighton Dome, because in my head I just associated the place with major stars – and certainly not me!

But this was a *big* tour, doing theatres, and I needed much bigger productions. I had lasers and big screens behind me showing my videos, plus all kinds of other stuff.

There is and always has been a hard core of Mayniacs who I recognise because they are at every gig I do, waiting outside and then right down in front of the stage. I know a lot of them by sight and quite a few by name as well – although I'd better not name them in this book in case I forget someone! By the time I began this tour they'd had a million pictures taken of them with me, but I will happily do a million more and I always make the time to say hi because without them I am nothing.

Although I truly loved that tour, I have to say that life on the road is hard. You're always eating random food at random times of the day and sleeping odd hours.

I pretty much partied in every city after every gig because – well – that's what you do! You're so buzzing after coming offstage that you want to go out and celebrate.

This time round I had a tour bus, so me and the band spent a lot of time in the back playing FIFA on Xbox.

As I was staying out all night partying, I'd get up in the early afternoon, then head to Nando's with the band. After eating we'd go into the soundcheck at the venue, get ready and then begin our set at about 9 p.m. Afterwards it was party time again until the early hours.

We slept on the bus for the whole tour and I really enjoyed the vibrations of the engine as I was trying to drop off – they kind of rocked me to sleep!

I have to admit I feel sorry for whoever used that bus after us because we made a serious mess of it. Including the crew, there were twelve guys sleeping on it, so it was really smelly. The chill-out room just stank of sweat, beer and late nights!

But having Anth and George there was brilliant and my other Brighton mates came to both the Brighton show and the London one, which, as I've said, was just insane.

When I went to meet my parents out by the toilets at the London show, I was mobbed and it got out of control. I had to give up on trying to speak to them and instead we arranged to meet in a cupboard behind the bar. Even then, on the way there from backstage, with five security guys around me, I felt this hand grabbing at me. I tried to shake it loose but when I looked around I realised it was my mum!

It was almost as bad for my brother Jack. When he walked out to say hello to our folks, all the fans mobbed him too, trying to get their picture taken with him.

Yeah, my headline tour is an experience I will never forget, and again I want to say thank you very much to all my fans for being there with me and making it happen.

During 2012 I'd been working on breaking the American market too. As an artist, breaking America is one of my biggest ambitions. When I went over there to start laying the foundations, my career was just kicking off in the UK and it was the height of the Brit Invasion that was going on in America. One Direction were blowing up there and Adele was huge.

So when my American label told me they loved 'Vegas Girl' and were going to go full force with it, I was over the moon. In the middle of the year I went to the States to do a radio tour, visiting loads of stations and talking to DJs, basically starting from scratch again, letting people know who I was and what I was about.

That took a long time as I went to every state and to some of the most random, out-there parts of the country. But one thing that soon became clear to me was that when people say they do things bigger in America, they are spot on. They made me feel like an absolute superstar. I was driven everywhere in blacked-out vehicles and when I arrived wherever I was going, there were more paparazzi than I had ever seen in my life.

'Vegas Girl' was my only release over there, so I was new to that audience, but there was a big buzz around me, with people talking about this kid from the UK with a Number One album being in the States. And this was boosted when my online fan base, originally started on YouTube, increased through Twitter and Facebook.

And on top of that, American Mayniacs would turn up at all the radio stations I was visiting, because they knew that when I visited their town it might be their only chance to meet me for a while.

'Vegas Girl' got added to all the key radio playlists and set us up brilliantly to release 'Turn Around' with Ne-Yo. That song went even bigger and radio stations all over the country really got behind it, no doubt helped by the fact it featured Ne-Yo, which meant my trips to and from the UK were very frequent as I tried to achieve success in two places at the same time.

In the States I did a lot of acoustic sets for radio, but I also did full-band showcases, the biggest being in New York, Atlanta and Los Angeles.

The hard work paid off because I got calls booking me on *Good Morning America* and *The David Letterman Show*, which was massive good news.

I also got to experience that whole side of celebrity culture that we don't have in the UK. The kind of thing that's on the celebrity-news website TMZ, where, as soon as you step out of a car, you are being videoed and people are asking questions with cameras thrust in your face.

But on the plus side, the most fun I had in America was the day they unveiled my bus for me. I had no idea what to expect, just that there was going to be some sort of surprise. And then I was taken around a corner and confronted with the Conor Maynard bus. It was huge and had my face plastered all over it. We ran a competition for Mayniacs to win the chance to go on the bus with me and we just drove around with me shouting through a megaphone, 'Check out my album *Contrast*!' and just being cheeky. I loved it.

While I was in America I saw Ne-Yo and he told me that every interview he was doing at the time was basically people asking him about me!

Then the really big news came in. MTV had booked me to perform in Times Square on New Year's Eve as a part of the celebrations. I couldn't believe it as it was a huge deal, but I was also a little upset because it meant celebrating New Year away from family and friends. But I did my best and flew Jack and Alex out to New York to be with me and the band.

We had the time of our lives, watching the confetti falling and being a part of that epic atmosphere. But I did make an absolute idiot of myself at one point. Traditionally a huge ball drops down for midnight and everyone cheers, so I was eager to see it happen. But, like a fool, I looked the wrong way and missed it. 'So when does the ball drop?' I asked, a minute after it had happened.

Contrast was released in America in January and went into the Top Forty, which for a first album by a UK artist is brilliant.

I came back just in time to release my new single, 'Animal', which features Wiley and is a song I'm very proud of. Funnily enough, I first bumped into Wiley at V Festival. A few weeks before the show, he had tweeted at me because his single 'Heatwave' had just come out and he'd said something about me flying past him in the charts and preventing him having a hit. So I'd tweeted back telling everyone to go out and buy his tune because I loved it.

When we actually met, he said he wanted to do a track with me, and I liked the idea. I'd been listening to this guy for years – remember the story I told you at the start of the book about that mate of mine getting the lyrics to 'Wearing My Rolex' all wrong? I kept my memories to myself – somehow telling Wiley that story didn't seem cool!

And now he wanted to do a song with me. I sent him 'Animal' and he was really feeling it and just threw some bars down on top of it.

A funny thing about that track is that the intro – when he's saying, 'Wiley, Conor Maynard, "Animal"' – was recorded on an iPhone because we'd forgotten to do that bit when he was recording his rap in the studio. So that's why it's got that kind of weird compressed sound to it – it's not a special effect!

When we shot the video for 'Animal' in November 2012 I took Anth and Alex along and Wiley noticed and was like, 'Yeah, man, always keep your mates with you to keep your feet on the ground.' I took that in and it reconfirmed what I'd had in my head since spending time with Ne-Yo and seeing how he was with his friends.

'Animal' went to Number Six in the charts and I think helped cement me as a proper artist who had really cutting-edge tracks. Along with 'Turn Around', it showed that I was more than a young lad making songs about partying.

Chapter Sixteen

RELATIONSHIPS

With so much happening to me in the last few years, one of the questions I get asked most often is how it affects my relationships with friends, family and girls.

Now, my relationship with my brother is very good. We are extremely close and I would say that we are best mates as all the fighting we used to do as kids has long since stopped. Jack loves all the madness that's come with my career and he gets a lot of the benefits of it as well. He's eighteen now and works for a company called Booked Magazine, which produces a magazine that is placed in schools to encourage kids to read. He does blogs for them on YouTube and they're getting really good views.

Jack is often in London hanging out with me, but we still don't really see as much of each other as we'd like to, with me being there and him being in Brighton. When we do meet, every couple of weeks, we make the most of it. And on our phones we have a constant group conversation between me, him, George and Alex, so one of us is always chipping in.

There's no jealousy between me and Jack, and I always try to look after him, because of course it's a difficult situation. People compare us and ask him, 'What have you done?' – which is unfair because what he does has nothing to do with me. He's got the spotlight on him – be it on Twitter or whatever – because of me and he hasn't asked for that. Sometimes he has to suffer on account of me in that I tell him to be careful about what he says to people or what opinions he puts on Twitter, because it all reflects back on me. I can understand why this could annoy him.

Then again, if he wants to party with me and come out to New York or be in my videos, that's the price he has to pay. Besides, there's nothing to stop him starting a new, anonymous Twitter account and talking about whatever he wants!

Obviously I love my little sister Anna, although since she's only twelve our relationship is very different from the one I have with Jack. She's pretty much just started secondary school and of course it's a bit weird for her as she has friends who badger her to call me, or whatever. But Anna's a clever girl and she knows how to handle things. Once a group of boys came over to her and went, 'Girls, girls, girls' right in her face, trying to wind her up. She said, 'You don't know my name, so I'm not going to speak to you,' and walked away, which I think is just brilliant.

It can be a bit funny meeting some of Anna's friends. My family's next-door neighbours' daughter is a friend of hers and every time I'm down in Brighton she wants a picture taken with me.

People get in touch with my mum too, asking for signed albums or signed anything, and on my behalf she almost always says yes. She tells me that she's had girls park outside the house, get out of the car and then take a picture of the place before driving off again. It's pretty hilarious that some people have found out my home address and just want a picture of where I grew up.

There was some tricky stuff for us as a family when I started getting known, and I think someone got hold of the wrong end of the stick when I did an interview with them. I said how amazing it was flying around the world, but that in the past our family holidays had been in caravan parks because my mum loved them. The story came out that I was from a deprived background and spent lots of my childhood on campsites! That was an odd one for us all to read.

I think the hardest thing for the family is when they read stories or articles which slate me. Countless times I've told my mum not to read about me, but she still takes every review personally and gets upset.

Just like my brother, sister and mum, my dad is very proud of me. After I'd signed my record deal I'd hardly seen him for about a week because he'd been working and I'd been in London. When I was back home he came into my room and gave me a big hug. Then he looked at me and said, 'I've been waiting to do that all week. I just want to say well done, this is amazing.'

That was a pretty emotional moment and I remember my eyes feeling very hot as I heard my dad congratulate me. He really respects people who go out and do something for themselves and he's so against laziness. I think that's probably a big part of why I am the way I am, always wanting to work hard and put in the time, because he's so proactive. Now that I've achieved something, I feel like I've grown even closer to my dad.

As a family we really make the most of our time together, and because we all meet up so infrequently, those moments are very valuable. But my parents still treat me like the same idiot I was before and don't let me get away with anything. I can't come home and play loud music without getting told off and I still have to do my chores, like take out the recycling or empty the rubbish bins.

What amuses, though, is that when I'm flicking through the TV hard drive I can see that they've recorded almost every programme that I've ever been on!

My friendships have developed over the last few years and I've built up a really close group of mates that I can trust. Samir – the boy I first made friends with at Saturday drama classes – is still a mate and I see him a lot. As it happens, he has the same birthday as my mate Alex.

I've really realised who my closest friends are since I signed my record deal and my life changed so wildly. They haven't turned against me or got jealous. They just understand what I have to do and that my life means that sometimes I'll be off the radar for a while.

But I don't feel bad about it, because they all know I will always make them a part of my success. That's why I have this phrase at the top of my Twitter profile: 'It's lonely at the top, that's why I plan to take you all with me.' And I truly mean it. I don't want to leave anyone behind, but in the meantime I have to get my head down and work.

When I'm with my friends I don't act differently from the way I always have, and they treat me just the same. If I'm being an idiot, they'll tell me. For example, there was a period when I was spending quite a lot of money without really thinking about the future. I'd splash out on stuff I didn't need, pick up all the drinks bills, pay for taxis or even flights for people I didn't really know, and generally say, 'Don't worry, it's on me.'

But Alex gave me a bit of a talking-to. 'Mate, you need to look after that money,' he said. 'This could all be over tomorrow and then you'll need this cash to keep you going.' Ever since then, he's refused to take anything off me. He'll point-blank refuse to come to London if he doesn't have the money to get here and pay for a night out, and he won't let me pay for him.

All of my friends are pretty protective of me, just like they are with everyone in our circle. If I meet someone new, it's almost like when a guy has to impress his new girlfriend's mates! They check the new person out, make sure they're cool and are really suspicious of their motives for ages – before they are willing to give the thumbs up to the newcomer. It can sometimes take up to a month before they accept that the new friend could actually be OK.

And then there are girls. From really early on – I'm talking aged five – I liked girls. There was this girl I saw on holiday at that age and I had some sort of fascination with her, which I didn't understand. My mum would teasingly ask if she was my girlfriend, which would obviously get a big no from me because everyone knows that when you are five, girls are disgusting! But that didn't stop me wanting to sit next to her in the sandpit and build castles.

Then, when I was ten or eleven, we had a prom at the end of Year Six and I danced with a girl for the first time, which felt good but really weird. I think she was probably my girlfriend for a day but then we broke up and I went back to playing football.

My first kiss was when I was thirteen, with a girl called Ellie who went to my drama school. She was definitely one of the best-looking girls in the class and I'd pretty much fancied her since I first saw her.

She was there full-time, unlike me, but she then started coming on Saturdays when I was there as well, which is how we met. We talked quite a lot at school, and then on MSN, and when we hung out in big groups of friends it was always me and Ellie that would end up sitting together and chatting.

One day I had a singing lesson and the two of us were the last ones in the line to go into class. Ellie held me back as if she wanted to talk to me. But then she looked at me in a way that let me know she wanted me to kiss her. Now, I'd never had a proper snog with anyone before, so I was really nervous and thinking, oh my God, what do I do?

I did my best and when we stopped kissing I wiped my mouth and could feel my heart going about a million beats per minute. I thought I was going to collapse. I think I enjoyed it, but I was so scared I was doing it wrong my knees were probably shaking.

Ellie went into the lesson ahead of me and I nipped to the toilet to try to get myself together and take a massive breath to steady my nerves. In the class afterwards I was still shaking for ages.

We started going out with each other, which basically meant that when we were all out with our friends, she and I would hold hands and have a kiss. We went out for about a month, which when you're thirteen is basically for ever.

Ellie wasn't only my first kiss – she was also the first girl ever to dump me! She ditched me over MSN and said she just didn't think we should be together any more. I went downstairs a little bit teary-eyed and told my mum that Ellie had been the one and that I would *never* find another girl. I was a bit upset about it, but somehow I lived!

I was always very comfortable around girls and while I was matey with boys, I did enjoy hanging around with girls because I was just basically flirting all the time.

After Ellie, I had a few little girlfriends here and there and girls were an important part of my life because, like any young lad, I was curious. I wanted to learn things about them and, well, find out about the kinds of things I could do with them that I couldn't do by myself, shall we say?

There were always guys showing off at school about what they'd done with this girl and that girl, and looking back on it, I'm sure almost all of it was untrue. But as a kid you believe it and I was always wondering if I was keeping up with what other people were getting up to.

It wasn't until Year Eleven, when I was sixteen, that I met my first proper girlfriend. Her name was Marina and we went out for almost the whole of that last year of school. She had a boyfriend already when I first started liking her and I took her to the cinema one day while she still had a boyfriend – as part of a big group – and I didn't know how to handle it because obviously she wasn't single.

But on the day she broke up with him, she called me five minutes later in tears to tell me about it. Obviously I was saying, 'I'm so sorry. This is awful news,' while inside quietly celebrating.

Marina said I was the first person she wanted to talk to and I took that as a good sign. We started going out soon after that and I was *properly* into her.

We were still very young, but I would say that was my first almost adult relationship. She was the first girl I took home to meet my parents and they really liked her. She was a very sweet girl, so I was really excited with the summer holidays ahead, because I'd never had a girlfriend during the summer before. I was really looking forward to hanging out with her and spending loads of time together.

We got halfway through the summer, having a great time going to the beach and just chilling. And then out of the blue she broke up with me. Over MSN –again! – after nine months! She said she couldn't do it to my face because she felt too bad. She said it just wasn't working – that was her excuse.

I knew something was up because I'd noticed she'd been talking to this other guy at our school and sending him texts. I used to joke about it, asking if she wanted to be with him instead of me and she'd laugh and tell me to shut up.

But the answer was actually yes! Two weeks after she finished with me, she was going out with him.

And we all went back to the same college after the summer, so I had to see them in the common room acting like a proper couple, holding hands and everything.

I was gutted. Everyone knew and kept talking to me about it. It was really horrible and I was so upset – but I refused to cry about it.

Chapter Seventeen

'MARY GO ROUND'

My next girlfriend was Marisha, who I'd met when I was fifteen and in Year Ten, when she first came to our school.

She was very hot and quickly became friends with the popular girls and would go for smokes during breaks and that kind of thing. But before she'd got in with them, I was one of the first people to start talking to her, because she sat behind me in English and I turned around and started chatting to her.

I tried to crack a few jokes, but she clearly wasn't that bothered and after a few weeks she'd started making friends and she used to do this thing which, looking back, was really cruel to me but is also quite hilarious.

She'd get me to walk her to the field to hang out, because she said she didn't know anyone. I'd happily walk with her for the chance to talk. But when we got there, she'd see her friends and say, 'All right, bye, Conor,' and leave me standing there by myself like a muppet!

I soon realised there was no way it was happening and gave up.

Cut forward two years to the first year of college and we ended up in the same form.

At the end of Year Eleven I had performed in front of the school and I'd had that comment from another girl saying that some of the other girls were talking about how hot I was. Well, it turns out Marisha was one of those girls! We started having a bit of a laugh in lessons and getting on well together and she always took the mickey out of me, calling me a nerd, because I was quite clever in class.

We had been in such different groups of friends for the last year or so that I never even considered there could be more to it than that. Then, on my seventeenth birthday, I went to someone's house party and Marisha was there. We ended up chatting all night and that led to a very unexpected kiss, which I had not seen coming at all.

She messaged me the next day saying, 'Maybe we shouldn't tell anyone that happened,' because we'd both had a couple of drinks and she wasn't sure if it meant anything. It would have been really awkward because we really were friends and everyone would have been like, 'You two?!'

But that kiss had definitely changed things, and when it snowed a few days later we all had a day off college and everyone met up in the park, which led to the two of us spending the whole day chatting together again.

We realised that we liked each other quite a lot and slowly we started to become a couple, without even really intending to. It just kind of happened.

It was on Marisha's birthday, 8 January, that we actually officially became boyfriend and girlfriend. She was the first girl that my parents ever allowed to stay at my house for the night and that was actually before we were officially together, which is probably how I got away with it! I told my parents we were just friends and of course we stayed in different beds.

I was really into Marisha, who'd done so much more than me, drinking, smoking and all that kind of thing, long before I'd even know people did that stuff. We were so different that my mates really questioned us being together, but for some reason it worked.

We saw a lot of each other, stayed at each other's houses and went out for meals together. We did everything that adults do in a real, grown-up relationship.

It was great for a while, but then that summer of 2011 was when my YouTube videos started to blow up a bit and I began getting messages from people and girls getting in touch. Straight away it was clear that the female attention I was getting really bothered her.

She wanted to know why girls were adding me on Twitter or if I knew who some girl was who was commenting on my Facebook page. She would get really wound up and angry about girls saying suggestive things to me and she'd want me to tweet them back and tell them to leave me alone, which I obviously couldn't do.

Marisha did try to be understanding, but she just could not stand it. You remember the first song I wrote, 'I Love You', the one that my dad was worried someone might try to steal? That was about her and is still up on YouTube.

I also started travelling to and from London all the time then as well, to meet labels and managers, which was exciting but meant I didn't see quite so much of Marisha. When I signed my deal with Parlophone, we were together and she was really chuffed and was at the celebratory dinner we all went out for. But she really struggled when I began spending more and more time in London recording or working with the Invisible Men, because she didn't understand why I didn't know what time I'd be finished in the studio. When I'd say I had no idea what time I could call her, she'd say, 'What are you *really* doing? Are you *really* finishing work at 1 a.m.?'

I tried to go back as often as I could and pay her surprise visits, but it was a big strain on the relationship that I was always away. Even so, we went through a lot together, both good and bad – passing our driving tests together and just finding out about life.

On the darker side, we went out one night in Brighton and we were attacked by a man who mistook us for some kids who had jumped him outside his restaurant and then run away. He'd started chasing them, came round a corner and thought we were them. So he kicked me in the chest. When Marisha jumped in and shouted at him, he hit her in the face in a blind rage.

The two of us ended up having to go the police station together. All these things we went through together meant we did have a proper bond.

Marisha and I had our differences and arguments, but we got on and she was a good girlfriend to me and she really did try to understand how my life was changing. I don't think any other girl could have coped better, especially when we were so young.

We tried hard to make it work, though, and she even came out to America with me to stay with Anth and his family in the summer of 2011. That was great, but it was also the beginning of the end for us.

We'd been arguing a lot beforehand, though we were hoping that the break in the States would help us make things right again. But we argued loads out there as well and when we came back I think we both knew that the end was coming.

Shortly afterwards I had to go back to the States on my own to spend a month recording, and when we got back the label wanted me to move up to London. That kind of triggered something in my head and I knew that I needed to end our relationship before I left Brighton. It was so hard trying to work out how to say that, but I knew I had to. Marisha and I were going to end anyway. We were arguing all the time and we had lost whatever we once had. I really did want it to work, but it had run its course and we'd have ended up hating each other if we had gone on much longer.

I knew that if I moved to London, she stayed there a few times and then we broke up, everything I'd see in my new place would remind me of her and I wanted a clean break and a fresh start. I didn't want memories of her in the room as I sat there alone.

So one day I took her to Brighton beach and sat her down to explain that I was moving and that we had to break up. It was horrible watching her crying, but we both knew it was coming and that one of us had to man up and say it out loud. I was the one moving away, so I felt I had to say it.

I guess we dealt with the situation in different ways. I was working so much that it made it easier for me to lose myself in what I was doing and not dwell on the sadness of it, so I was the lucky one. I could also express my feelings through music and I actually wrote a song on the album about Marisha – 'Mary Go Round'. I chose Mary because the name is similar to hers and she knew it was about her.

She had to stay in Brighton without all the excitement I had going on and was just miserable, which I thought was really unfair, so after the split we still talked and stayed in touch. But in the end that wasn't a good idea and led to me writing 'Run Away Love', a song which basically says we can't keep talking as it will only make things worse for us both.

Every time we talked it brought all the feelings back. I'd hear that she was seeing someone new and it would hurt me or she'd hear that I had been seeing someone and it would make us both so upset.

So I told her I couldn't talk to her any more. I was in tears and it really hurt me to do it, but if we kept talking then neither of us would properly get over it.

After that, Anth came to stay with me in London and he was really there for me when I was going through it. He was a shoulder for me to lean on and gave me the strength to not text or call Marisha.

Eventually things moved on and now we occasionally say hi to each other and things are civil, but that's it. I'll always look back on that time and have happy memories, and she definitely shaped who I am today as a massively important part of my life. She taught me how to be a man, take responsibility and stop being a kid.

But that's it – memories. There are definitely no feelings left.

Chapter Eighteen

THE PRICE OF FAME

Since I split with Marisha and turned eighteen, things have changed for me a lot in terms of relationships with girls and friends. Fame has a strange effect on a lot of the girls I meet and I had a few mini relationships early on, but nothing lasted because I realised it just doesn't work unless you are massively committed to each other. I am always away, they don't understand what my life is like and I don't have the time to give them what they deserve.

Don't get me wrong, I've had fun and I've enjoyed dating, but then there are the ones who aren't all they seem. I was seeing one girl for a little while who was never that interested in me or what I was doing – until I told her I was going into the studio to work with Pharrell Williams! Then she was all over me. It *could* have just been a coincidence, but that thought was always in the back of my head and it made me so paranoid about what girls wanted from me. With every girl I speak to now, I wonder if they're really interested in me, or is it what I do that they like?

It's hard and I guess sometimes you've just got to believe in people and give them the benefit of the doubt. There have even been a few celebrities – naming no names – who have mentioned that we have been together and I've never even done anything with them!

It's kind of scary because when it comes to girls I never know who I can trust. That's a price I pay for the job I have. That's the downside. I've come to rely a lot more on my close friends as a kind of barometer to back up my instincts with girls I meet. They won't let me get too carried away with someone in a club and remind me that I have to keep my head screwed on properly.

I've had a few occasions where I've met girls I've really liked – even just as friends – and I've had to walk away from them, because I just know it can't work. Girls I wish I'd met later in my life when things have calmed down a bit and I can actually spend the time I want with them. I wrote a song on *Contrast* called 'Just In Case', which is about one of those girls that I had to let go because I knew it was just the wrong time in my life to be with her. Basically it's telling her that if things go wrong with her new man one day, let me know because maybe I'll be in the right place to give her everything by then.

The whole job makes relationships in general difficult. Sometimes it's just geography. Allura – the girl who was in the video for 'Vegas Girl' – is a lovely girl and a totally amazing friend, but she lives in New York, so I can only ever see her when I'm out there. It was really upsetting saying goodbye to her after that trip and I took her to a basketball game to say goodbye, realising that here was someone I really connected with who wasn't going to be a part of my life. I suppose it gives me plenty to write about in songs at least!

Sometimes – and there's no other way of saying this – shit happens. Whether it's your fault or not, life is life and relationships go wrong. I've lost friends – even my closest friend, Anth. We got so close doing our covers and one of the best things about signing my deal at the end of 2010 was getting to meet him face to face for the first time when they flew him over and he stayed with my family and me in Brighton.

We worked in a little studio down there, enjoying ourselves, and went to the same sandwich shop every day – Tom's Deli. It snowed one day and I think that was the first time Anth, being from Virginia, had ever seen snow, and he hated how cold it was. He found it really weird that we drove on the left side of the road, and he kept saying, 'Man, you drive stick, you drive stick,' which is the Americans' really odd way of saying you drive a manual car. All of their cars are automatic, so you just point and go.

Anth fitted in really well with my Brighton mates – especially Alex – and we genuinely did become best friends. As I mentioned before, I even went out, along with Marisha, to stay with him and his family for two weeks in 2011. We met his family, who couldn't speak any English at all but were really welcoming to me.

As I write this now, I'm still sad that Anth and I are no longer friends. I fought for that friendship and so did he. Certain people got upset when he went all over America with me on my promo trips, because articles started appearing that suggested we were a double act and it was just supposed to be all about me. But there was no way I was going to not have him with me, because he was my best friend and being in America was the only chance I had to see him.

We were always there for each other at big moments in our lives, be it on Skype, on the phone or in the same, physical place. But at the start of 2013 something very real went wrong between us and destroyed that friendship. Now I'll always look back at what we had and wonder if my best friend was my best friend for the wrong reasons. I try not to believe that, and good people do make mistakes, but that thought is there.

I hope that one day we can put our differences behind us, overcome things and be as close again as we once were. Time is a great healer.

EPILOGUE

So now it's autumn 2013 and I'm gearing up for my new album. One of the things I learned from making *Contrast* was that the songs you write dictate how people will see you.

I loved 'Can't Say No' and 'Vegas Girl' and they are great songs that really represent my young, fun side. But it wasn't until 'Turn Around' and 'Animal' came out that people started to see me as a potentially more mature artist. I've grown up a lot in the last two years and I want to show what I've learned – and my fans have grown with me.

In the new album I need to show that, and I've really given people more of me in the songs I've written for it, rather than writing tongue in cheek. I've got much more to say now and I think my voice has improved a lot because I've been singing so much. I've dug a lot deeper and shown a lot more.

On this album I've definitely addressed my relationships with girls and all the relationships I've had in my life since I found success in music and everything changed.

The cheekiness of my character still comes through in some of the songs, but I wanted a more adult, darker feel to others, as I've grown up a lot.

I feel like I have more to offer in the studio now as well, because I'm not just some kid making my first album. I have experience in writing songs and I'm more confident in my ideas.

I want to give my fans something special as it's all about them really. They were there before my record label and before I was on TV and I will never forget that.

I'm also going to do my best to see as much of my family as possible and keep my friends closer than ever.

So far 2013 has been hectic and I've been writing and recording constantly, both in the UK and America. I'm experiencing the festival circuit this year, doing all kinds of gigs, including Wireless, and headlining my European tour.

My dream is at some point to headline the O2 Arena in London and sell it out after having a Number One album around the world.

As time goes on I'm also hoping to do a lot more charity stuff. Every time I've done any charity work, I've always felt really good afterwards because I hope that – as I sit there with someone really ill – I've maybe been able to help them forget for even a moment what they are going through. I especially want to get involved with charities for kids as obviously I'm young myself and my fan base is predominantly young too. If I ever get to the point where I can put a lot of money into a charity, or organise something big to raise awareness, then I will be really happy.

I've worked really hard, but I've also been incredibly lucky to find success in a job which is also my passion.

Forget the fame, so many people don't have the chance to pursue what they love and I feel like I have to appreciate my blessings constantly.

To have come so far in so few years – from a small stage in Brighton to having millions of fans – still blows my mind and fills me with pride and gratitude.

My outlook on life is to enjoy every moment for what it is – be it meeting someone new, writing a melody or just listening to a new song for the first time. The future is unknown for everyone, so I live for right now and try to keep a smile on my face.

101

I can see forever from

long as as we're together

HORUS

sa Around.

oaking so high up off

oaking so high,

sa Around,

I'm, I out let go,

we go again,

dream is over, I'm a

chorus

take it,

make it

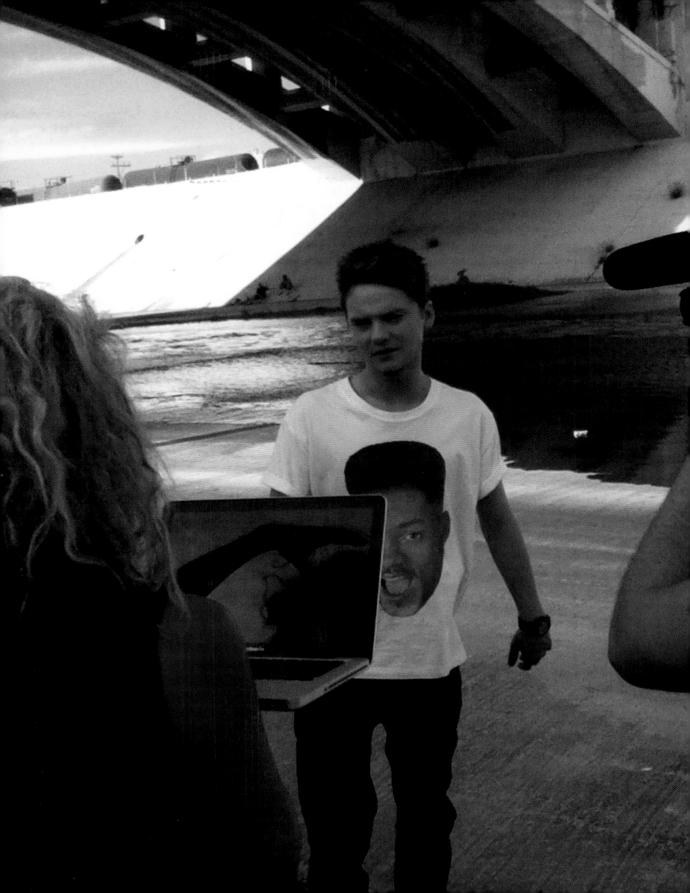

shed some tears since

the nothing,

osed to remember?

s,

jade baby,

on show to my kids,

and my mind is telling

CONOR ⬛ MAYNARD

Animal
Take off
Talk
Vegas Girl
Talk
Mary go round
Pictures
Talk
Drowning
Starships
Diamonds
Quick Talk
Just in case
Lift Off
Quick talk
Glass Girl
Talk
Headphones
Better than you
<u>EnCore</u>
Can't say no
Turn around

res.

I didn't wanna miss o

he how could take the p

you knew they were w

left,

were part our history, th

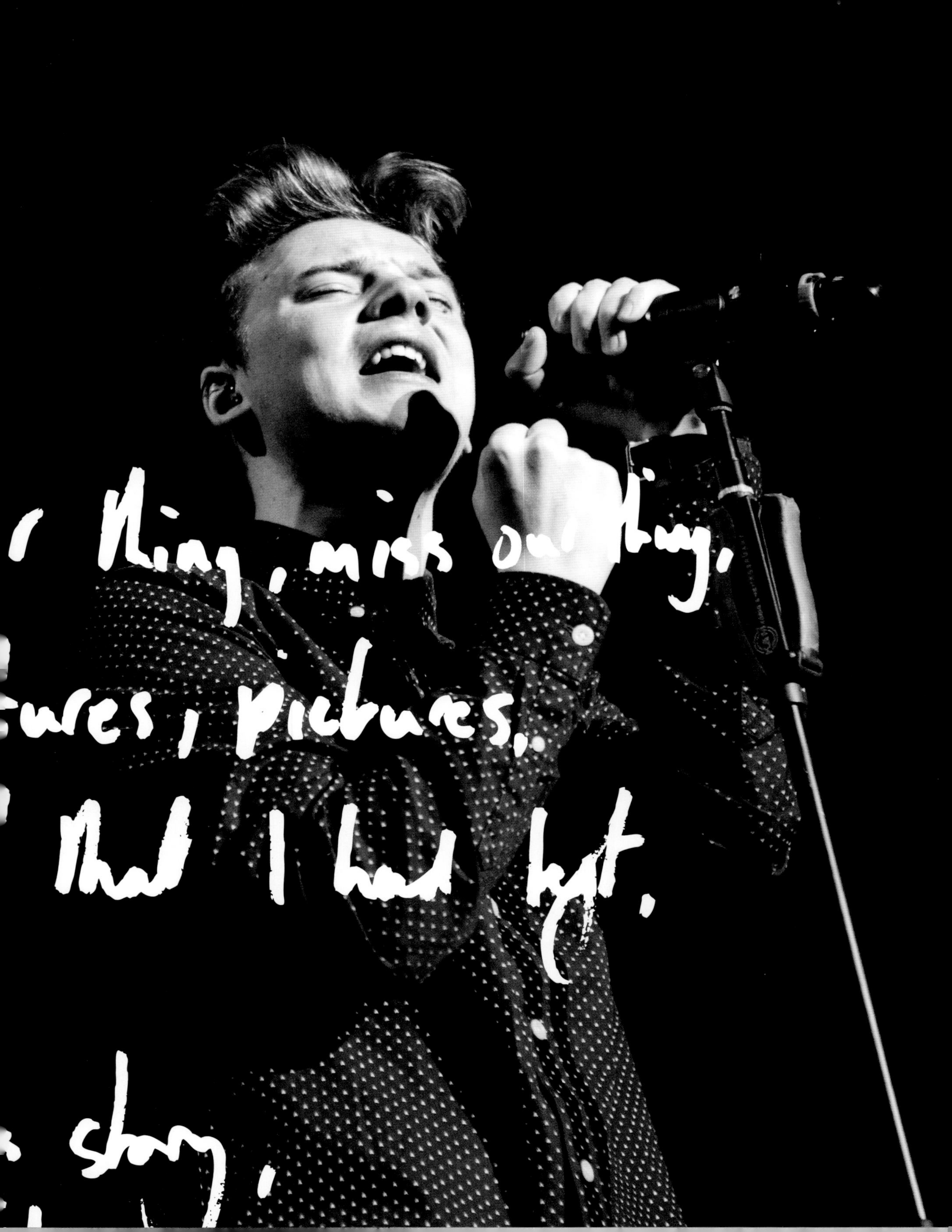

miss
pictures,
I had

I
close
your eyes. look at me
around.
I've got you, we won't
or see forever from up
here as we're together

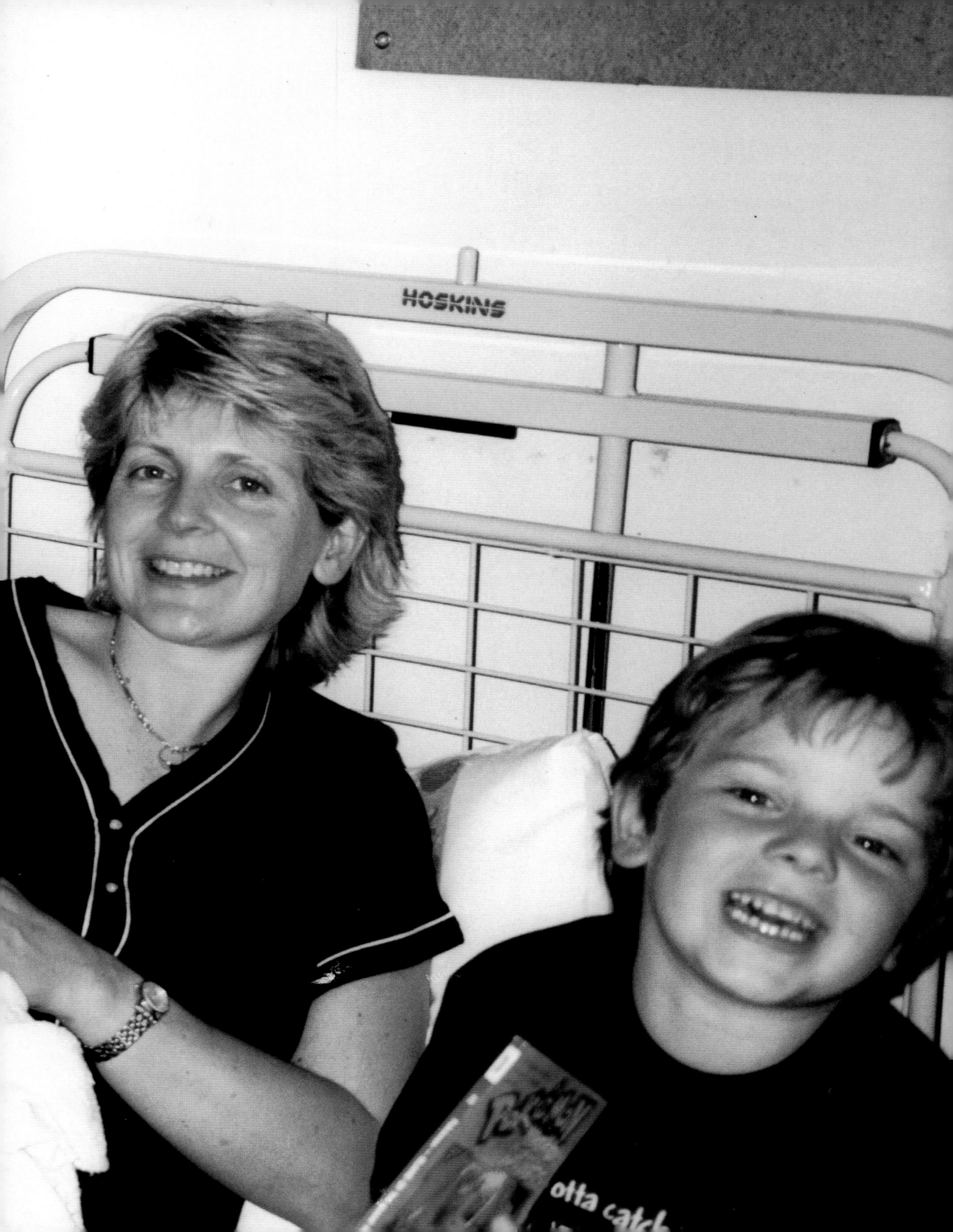
HOSKINS

GVA Grimley

International Property Advisers

VISITOR

CONOR MAYNARD

Host: **DREAM TEAM**
DT

Valid On: **29/09/2005**

Signature

Conor Maynard

Your signature indicates your awareness of the Safety

Acknowledgements

MAYNIACS!!!!... WOW! I can't believe what a mad ride this past year has been for me; releasing my first ever album, and getting to travel around the world and meet some of you amazing lot along the way. And now I have my first book! Crazy! I hope you enjoy reading this as much as I did putting it together. Going through all of the photos for the book was fun and a trip down memory lane! Oh! And don't judge some of my dodgy choices of outfits as a kid; I was clearly a leader in fashion! ;-)

There are so many people I'd like to thank for helping me put this idea into reality and into your hands. My family – Mum, Dad, Jack and Anna, you have been by my side through it all and I couldn't have done it without your constant love and support, so thank you!

Joe Mott – thank you for listening to me ramble on for days on end and not falling asleep in the process!

My management team at Turn First Artists – Aaron, Cassandra, Sarah and Alan. Thank you for everything you do for me, you always go that extra mile and have my back. Also, a big thank you to Alan for helping put this all together with me these past 6 months, it's not been an easy job I know, but we got there in the end!

Miles Leonard, Elias Christidis, Mandy Plumb, Dan Sanders, Rob Owen, William Luff, Kate Hiscox, Emmy Lovell, Tina Skinner, Dave Rajan, Martin Finn, Jason Bailey and my Entire Parlophone Music crew, thank you for everything you have helped me achieve this past year – we've only just begun!

To my band, (who you pretty much see as much of as me these days) thanks for the laughs on those loooong road trips! Big shout out to Mark Pickard too for everything he does for me on the road and making it all run so smoothly.

A big thank you to my Hodder family for making this book actually happen! Especially Charlotte Hardman, Mark Booth, Fiona Rose, Bea Long, Eleni Lawrence and all the team there for working so hard behind the scenes, and a special thanks to Joby Ellis for making the book look so great!

Chloe Wright and all at Harbottle & Lewis, Pat Savage and Ryan Polson at OJK – thank you for your patience in this project and doing your part making it happen.

To all my MAYNIACS around the world. Thank you for your constant love and support it really does mean everything to me and I couldn't do what I love to do which is record music and stand up on that stage and perform if it wasn't for each and every one of you.

See you in a bit... Conor x

96-97 David Titlow photo shoot

98-99 Conor and brother Jack / Fans on Conor UK headline tour

100-101 Brian Higbee photo shoot, Los Angeles

102-103 Photo shoot / Vegas Girl video shoot, New York

104-105 In the studio with Pharrell Williams, Miami

106-107 Conor with brother Jack and sister Anna / Jesse Jenkins photo shoot, Brighton

108-109 Jesse Jenkins photo shoot

110-111 Conor and Ne-Yo, Ne-Yo UK Tour

112-113 Jesse Jenkins photo shoot, Brighton

114-115 Conor / Conor meeting fans at a performance

116-117 Conor and band, backstage on Ne-Yo Tour

118-119 Conor and band, backstage on Ne-Yo Tour

120-121 Conor tour bus written on by fans while on tour / Much Music Awards, Canada

122-123 Turnaround video shoot, Los Angeles / Brian Higbee photo shoot, Los Angeles

124-125 Conor and fans, Paris train station / David Titlow photo shoot, London

126-127 Brian Higbee photo shoot, Los Angeles

128-129 Jesse Jenkins photo shoot, Brighton

130-131 Jesse Jenkins photo shoot / Conor and brother Jack

132-133 Conor / Brian Higbee photo shoot

134-135 Ne-Yo UK Tour

136-137 Capital Summetime Ball, Wembley Stadium / Lytham Proms performance 2013 / Conor and Vegas Girl - Vegas Girl video shoot, New York

138-139 David Titlow photo shoot, London / New York skyline

140-141 Conor and Ne-Yo, backstage on Ne-Yo Tour

142-143 Conor, brother Jack and family friend Ellis

144-145 Conor thank-you note to fans / Ne-Yo UK Tour

146-147 Conor and Tyler The Creator backstage in Miami / Tour bus / Conor, Kylie, Gabby Roslin – Silver Clef Awards, London / Conor & Ludacris, in the studio with Pharrell, Miami

148-149 T4 On The Beach performance / Tour setlists

150-151 Soundcheck on Ne-Yo Tour

152-153 Conor and Richard Branson, Vancouver, Canada / Turn Around video shoot, Los Angeles

154-155 Conor drum skin

156-157 Ne-Yo Tour / Jesse Jenkins photo shoot, Brighton

158-159 Vegas Girl video shoot, New York

224-225 Conor and 100m US sprinter Tyson Gay at 2012 London Olympics / Fans on red carpet

226-227 Brian Higbee photo shoot, Los Angeles / David Titlow photo shoot, London

228-229 Conor and Ne-Yo performing Turn Around, Ne-Yo UK Tour

230-231 Virgin Atlantic Performance, Vancouver, Canada / Conor and fans, radio promo tour UK / Conor fans waiting outside Shepherds Bush Empire, London

232-233 Jesse Jenkins photo shoot, Brighton

234-235 Conor, Jack, Mum & Dad at Anna's birth

236-237 With John Barnes / Dream Team pass / Brian Higbee photo shoot, Los Angeles

238-239 Jesse Jenkins photo shoot / Conor and Ne-Yo in the studio, Los Angeles

INDEX OF PICTURES

240-241 Ne-Yo UK Tour

242-243 Jesse Jenkins photo shoot, Brighton

244-245 Conor, Ne-Yo UK Tour

First published in Great Britain in 2013 by Coronet

An imprint of Hodder & Stoughton

An Hachette UK company

1

Photography: Jesse John Jenkins, Brooke Nipar, David Titlow, Brian Higbee

Personal Photos supplied by: Conor Maynard, Helen Maynard, Aaron Hercules,

Conor McDonnell, Virgin Atlantic Press Office, Nordof Robbins

Book design: Joby Ellis

Editorial input: Alan Jewell

Conor Maynard is represented exclusively by Turn First Artists – www.turnfirstartists.com

A CIP catalogue record for this title is available from the British Library

ISBN 978 1 444 77848 9

Printed in Germany by Mohnmedia Mohndruck GmbH, Gütersloh

Hodder & Stoughton policy is to use papers that are natural, renewable and recyclable products and made from wood grown in sustainable forests. The logging and manufacturing processes are expected to conform to the environmental regulations of the country of origin.

Hodder & Stoughton Ltd

338 Euston Road

London NW1 3BH

www.hodder.co.uk